MW01000413

Praise for *Gentle Power*

"Nobody has taught me more about sisu than Emilia Elisabet Lahti. In this beautiful book, Elisabet shows us how strength and toughness are not the same thing. A much-needed antidote to the myth of mind over matter, and a touching, honest story of one woman's journey to discover the true origins of grit and fulfillment."

—ANGELA DUCKWORTH, PhD, MacArthur Fellow, Rosa Lee and Egbert Chang Professor at the University of Pennsylvania, and *New York Times* bestselling author of *Grit: The Power of Passion and Perseverance*

"This captivating and heartfelt book invites readers on a compelling journey to their fullest expression of power and leadership."

—EMMA SEPPÄLÄ, PhD, Yale School of Management, author of *The Happiness Track*

"A beautiful book written by one of the most important voices in positive psychology. Part balm and part rallying call, this book is a deep well for the weary positive champions who are searching for a way to transform the lives of others and to discover a more powerful path to an empowered, connected, and hopeful world."

—SHAWN ACHOR, *New York Times* bestselling author of *Big Potential* and *The Happiness Advantage*

"*Gentle Power* is a brilliant and refreshing idea. Lahti is a rare combination of real-life adventurer and scientist. With the warmth and authenticity typical to her writing, she outlines an inviting path toward our highest expression through the power of everyday relationships."

—SCOTT BARRY KAUFMAN, PhD

"Lahti examines how attachment styles can be employed to understand ourselves and others with more compassion and thereby assist us into evolved forms of leadership. Throughout *Gentle Power*, Lahti kindly nudges us toward bold self-inquiry and genuine, life-changing empowerment."

—DIANE POOLE HELLER, PhD, author of
Crash Course, The Power of Attachment,
and *Healing Your Attachment Wounds*

"Emilia Elisabet Lahti is a pioneering researcher and rising star in the new human potential movement. *Gentle Power*, her first book, is a bold invitation into what's possible as a human being. Infused with a powerful combination of backbone, heart, and original research, Lahti gently but persuasively challenges readers to question perceived limitations and, ultimately, transform barriers into frontiers."

—JOSHUA STEINFELDT, host of *The Courageous Life*
podcast, mindfulness teacher, and professional coach

GENTLE

A Revolution in How We Think,
Lead, and Succeed Using the
Finnish Art of **Sisu**

POWER

EMILIA ELISABET LAHTI, PhD

sounds true
BOULDER, COLORADO

Sounds True
Boulder, CO 80306

Published 2023

Book design by Charli Barnes

Printed in the United States of America

BK06478

Names: Lahti, Elisabet, author.
Title: Gentle power : a revolution in how we think, lead, and succeed /
    Emilia Elisabet Lahti.
Description: Boulder, CO : Sounds True, 2023. | Includes bibliographical
    references.
Identifiers: LCCN 2022037005 (print) | LCCN 2022037006 (ebook) | ISBN
    9781683649694 (hardback) | ISBN 9781683649700 (ebook)
Subjects: LCSH: Resilience (Personality trait) | Leadership. |
    Determination (Personality trait) | Control (Psychology)
Classification: LCC BF698.35.R47 L34 2023 (print) | LCC
    BF698.35.R47 (ebook) | DDC 155.2/4--dc23/eng/20220830
LC record available at https://lccn.loc.gov/2022037005
LC ebook record available at https://lccn.loc.gov/2022037006

10 9 8 7 6 5 4 3 2 1

FSC
www.fsc.org
MIX
Paper | Supporting
responsible forestry
FSC® C103098

To Stephane Leblanc (1966–2021), whose grace, generosity, and gentle sisu were an inspiration for this book. In Stephane's words, "Love is the most powerful force there exists in this world."

We are fierce warriors, gentle nurturers, and everything in between.

—PETER LEVINE[1]

Contents

CONTENTS

Preface:
An Invitation to Gentle Power

Love is our base element of life, and love has always been there waiting for us to remove the veils that conceal it. Power is our base element too, and together with love, it lays the blueprint for how we express our energy and potential in life. I call their harmonious expression *gentle power.*

This book is the result of my lifelong struggle to learn about love and power through trial and error. It comes out of my quest to discover how to show up for myself and others from a place of kindness while not disowning my boundaries and self-worth. This pursuit to become more resolute yet loving—and more loving yet resolute—has brought me to the edge of my capacity, curiosity, and courage more times than I can count.

The truth is, I'm still learning. And often it feels like I'm failing as much as I succeed. But I've noticed that when I change my perspective to focus less on *achievement* and more on *learning*, something shifts in the narrative. In that new paradigm, every failure I meet—just like any ecstatic moment of reckoning—reveals itself as a lesson in love and power.

My quest has taken me on a run across an entire country in search of both my shadowy pain points and the parts of me where the light already shines. It has also transported me to faraway lands to gain perspective through the ancient wisdom of martial arts in a remote mountain temple. My quest has called me to overcome my crippling fear of public embarrassment by stepping onto the global stage as a speaker, and it has found me shattered into pieces by what I mistakenly thought was love. My quest has seen me transcend the trauma of interpersonal violence and has witnessed me gain the courage to love and trust again.

Over time, I've learned to take full responsibility for creating the future I want to manifest by standing behind my vision to discover my sovereignty as the protagonist of my own story. All my so-called failures have led to this. Instead of following someone else's drumbeat, I've learned to transcend the naïve uninitiated psyche of my youth that confused entanglements for authentic relationships, that mistook self-importance for self-worth. Ultimately, my quest sent me on whatever path it took to discover the union of hard and soft within myself. From that space of gentle power, I was finally able to begin building a true and honest union with others.

At its core, this book is about discovering and managing love and power. As a fundamental ingredient in our lives, power is exchanged in every conversation we have, in every traffic encounter, and in every message we share. Every behavior, gesture, thought, and word has the ability to *em*power or *disem*power. Like love, power is not an abstraction, but more of an active verb. How we express that verb is our contribution to the world. It's our legacy lived in the here and now, and it ultimately requires us to step more fully into our maturity.

For a long time, I was a passionate human rights activist who put immense effort into convincing everyone about the importance and urgency of compassion, personal responsibility, and justice. I actively shared my ideas and advice on social media, and I facilitated women's empowerment circles to contribute to community building. My concern for humanity kept me going in the day, but it also kept me up at night. I was so consumed by the injustice and suffering I witnessed in the world that my partner at the time proposed I take a break—just one day a week (Friday) when I didn't doomscroll or ask people to sign petitions or post on Facebook. My instructions were simply to enjoy being alive. He called it *No Rant Friday*. In truth, I think No Rant Friday was more for him than me. No matter how beautiful the intention, it can get heavy to spend time with people who always carry the world on their shoulders. As I'll demonstrate later, the weight we take on in life has everything to do with our boundaries, our relationship to power, and even our experience of love.

Our deepest strengths have everything to do with gentleness toward ourselves and others.

In recent years—along with my newly discovered gentleness toward myself and others—I've learned to let go of my need to be right and constantly work to make the world a better place. I've also learned to let go of thinking of myself as a teacher or an expert per se. From where I stand, the best I can do is keep working on myself and encouraging others. In the daily ebb and flow of contraction and expansion, I trust that I'm continuing to learn, grow, and heal those parts in me that stand in the way of my ability to love and care for others. Throughout everything, I'm writing it down and sharing the stories. This book is one of those stories.

The run I mentioned a few paragraphs back was a fifteen-hundred-mile solo jaunt across New Zealand. My initial goal was to complete the trip in fifty days—completing more than a marathon each day with my trusted one-person crew taking care of my practical needs, such as food and so on. Needless to say, it was an extremely intimate, isolated experience that tested the boundaries of my physical and mental fabric and required around two years of preparation. The run was also the fieldwork portion of my doctorate thesis on *sisu*, which was then a somewhat lesser-known Finnish concept related to perseverance, inner fortitude, and the boundless human spirit. What I learned during those excruciating hours on the road by myself was life-altering. It now acts as the foundation for my personal life as well as my research into human behavior and consciousness. For centuries, sisu has been thought of as some superhuman resolve for never giving up. Surprisingly, my run across New Zealand taught me way more about surrender and suppleness than strict resolve and rigor. In fact, I learned that our deepest strengths may often have more to do with gentleness toward ourselves and others.

My run was also an opportunity to launch Sisu Not Silence, a movement that seeks to dismantle the shame that (unjustly so) tends to accompany the experience of interpersonal violence—be the abuse emotional, physical, or sexual—and celebrates the strength of the millions who've overcome these atrocities. As a social scientist and overcomer myself, I noticed that people who suffer from domestic violence are often deemed weak, damaged, or even responsible for their trauma, which has everything to do with how people struggle to speak about these experiences. That's why together with several volunteers I organized the global Sisu Not Silence campaign. The campaign also included the journey across New Zealand with fifteen in-person events along my route to help inspire the creation of compassionate cultures with zero tolerance for abuse of any kind.

Sisu has many expressions, and some are even destructive. In its gentle-power form, sisu is ultimately a victory of pliability over pain or discernment over sheer determination. As much as I trained my body for the run, I had to train my mind to overcome certain deeply ingrained beliefs I harbored—beliefs like "progress requires pain," "there's inherent glory in suffering," and "achievement is all about mind over matter." In contrast, it was only through gentle power (or *warm sisu*, as I sometimes call it) that I was able to do what I did in New Zealand while still honoring myself, even under extreme pressure. I learned that accomplishing a goal at all costs wasn't for me, and the whole *mind over matter* mentality wasn't something I wanted to promote as a leader. Instead, I wanted to help others see that there is another way: *to align mind with matter.*

Life itself is the ultimate ultramarathon. The journey is varied and long, and it offers us countless chances to know ourselves, ease into our own true pace, and find confidence in the innate wisdom of our mind and body to carry us from rough terrain into the lush pastures of harmony. The questions I ended up asking myself during the run (for example, *What example am I setting through my decisions and the way I carry myself? How can I honor myself and others throughout this run? To what extent am I guided by mental autopilot based on old habits versus discerning the best course of action fresh in the moment?*) ultimately freed me from the tyranny of performance and obligation at the cost of presence. It was through contemplating these questions that I transcended my need to always try so hard (no matter what) and be right (no matter what). It felt as if I had found a portal into some lesser-explored fibers of my being—namely, the parts of me that inherently valued understanding over accomplishment, harmony over endless self-proving, and integrity over accolades.

Personal leadership is the most important gift we can give ourselves. It's also our most significant gift to the world because the ripples of our actions are more apparent and immediate in this era of a global digital community. On one hand, demeaning messages in online forums have had a hand in several tragic teenage suicides; on the other, people have leveraged social media to incite positive actions, like the Ice Bucket Challenge that helped the ALS Association raise over $115 million for research and elevated awareness of the disease. None of these outcomes just "happen." Behind them are people making choices based on their estimation of the value of human life, which means that both power and gentleness, as well as leadership, are core ingredients here. For better or worse, they all have an impact to the system.

The need for leadership and leadership development has never been more urgent than in today's uncertain, quickly evolving, and super-connected world. In part, this book is a call to redefine leadership not only in terms of titles and positions, but as a role in life as well as an ongoing responsibility. Shifting our leadership paradigm might sound like an overwhelming task, but we haven't arrived at the doorstep of this new era unprepared. We come fortified with the wisdom of cultures past and present, the hard-won lessons of other curious pilgrims of life, and the incomparable gifts of our own experience. Accordingly, this book is more descriptive than prescriptive. I want to offer the perspectives and practices that have worked for me, all while encouraging you to primarily reflect on your personal wisdom and experience to foster your own relationship with gentle power.

As Martin Luther King Jr. stated in 1967, "What is needed is a realization that power without love is reckless and abusive, and love without power is sentimental and anemic. Power at its best is love implementing the demands of justice."[1] It's my wish that this book encourages that realization and that it helps you understand the fundamental role of power in all human interactions. I also hope that it assists you in uncovering the potential for gentleness that resides within you.

Whether we're facing external peaks or internal valleys, our most inspiring qualities as humans are our courage and endurance to keep moving forward. This tendency of ours transforms former barriers into future frontiers, and things we once feared dissolve like the sublime dreamscape that fades with the sunrise. This is how we became what I sometimes like to call *Homo overcomus*. This is what sisu is all about—the eternal spark inside us that refuses to let us disappear. Gentle power takes it even further. It's the power of nurture and care for all living beings that turns that spark into something graceful, caring, patient, and sustaining.

I'm convinced that gentle power is the shift that's going to make the difference. Over the past decade or so, a tidal wave of research and literature on the benefits of compassionate leadership, communication soft skills, and psychological safety in teams and communities has been swelling, and it's about to hit the shore of our collective consciousness with undeniable power. I predict that one day we'll look back on the abundant examples of inflated egos and poor leadership in the public sphere (and all over social media) and cringe in utter disbelief at what we tolerated—and even glorified—for far too long.

This book is an invitation to learn from our collective journey as leaders. It's full of my stories but also those of various researchers, parents, entrepreneurs, teachers, friends, family members, and leaders of all types, whose wisdom and experience form part of the core foundation of this book. I hope you'll join us. Through your engaged involvement, this book becomes your story too.

Introduction

I t was my thirty-eighth birthday, and I was sitting on a wooden deck of a cottage in the Los Padres National Forest in California. Everything was still. The night sky was clear of clouds and dotted with a curious glow of stars peering at me from light-years away. The moment was abundant with a kind of storyless presence that stimulated my senses with soft alertness. Suddenly, the air around me turned dense, and I sensed an anticipation in the treetops towering above me like giants against the black November sky. It was as if something ancient had been making its way toward me for a long time and was now about to make its grand entrance. Then, a gust of wind brushed powerfully over the circle of redwoods around me and made everything above the ground sway. The moment of stillness had birthed itself into motion in a single breath, maturing into an observable power that made everything it touched shift, respond, and reorganize to adapt to its majestic emergence.

Before that moment, there had been a motion of a different kind— that of gentle awakening potential. I could feel it in the union of roots and wind. It was a nonchalant presence of a power so free from ambition and force that it didn't need to impose or coerce, nor did it need to apologize for its presence. Nature once more had shown me how gracefully the supple and substantial, tender and tough, and formidable and fragile can coexist, how they dance and blend in the most unsuspecting moments of our everyday existence. It also reminded me how good it feels to witness this kind of harmony and how much we need an awakening into such an existence.

Our world currently is creaking dangerously beneath the weight of past mistakes made in leadership (and followership, for that matter). We're facing a perfect storm of overlapping crises in public health, global markets, income disparity, the environment, family relationships, as well as displacement of entire populations and global conflict—at worst, escalating to wars. Our leaders have created systems that concentrate power and wealth in the hands of a small group of people while most of the world is kept in such emotional and economic distress that it leaves them little chance for anything more than basic survival.

It doesn't have to be this way. Human thought—when used without fear and for the benefit of all—is a thing of magic, and our planet holds the resources to sustain global well-being and create genius solutions beyond our wildest dreams. But it can only happen if we are organized around a common vision of unity. The tiniest unit of unity is the inner shift from *me* to *we,* and it means to optimize our leadership to empower each other in our everyday actions as well as on a grander scale. To empower means to support someone to have confidence in themselves and access to the resources (mental or material) they need to stand in their sovereignty. And we do this while knowing that when the people we empower discover a deeper experience of their strength and purpose, they may want things that no longer align with our preferred plan of action. This means giving our children full autonomy to choose their career path and support their choices of partners, or it might mean letting go, gracefully and kindly, of an intimate partner who wishes to part ways with us. At the heart of *true* leadership—even when its function is to guide and direct—always ultimately lies the intention for freedom and autonomy for the people we engage with.

The shadow of people wanting *to be leaders* without actually doing what's needed *to lead* has caught up with us. At the same time, the potential for something new—a kind of collective consciousness that values true leadership—has never felt so palpable. Individuals across the planet are becoming increasingly curious about disciplines that value presence, slowing down, self-inquiry, and interconnectedness. Practices that a couple of decades ago would have been unheard of outside of a few in-groups are now common (mindfulness and yoga among them) and included in the workplaces of some of the most influential companies in the world. Although the pace of this type of change might feel slow and unnoticeable in the larger picture, I believe it hints at the coming age—an age in which we leave behind outdated ways of relating to each other and step into a new realm of leadership and collaboration.

This book outlines a universal vision and strategy applicable to all domains of human interaction. I've spent the last years researching what I've termed gentle power—a kind of integrity-fueled fortitude that cultivates balance in both our strong and soft sides—and I propose that gentle power will restore balance in our world that has come to value competition over connection and profit over purpose and presence. No wonder so many of us feel lost and struggle to align with our potential when the message we mostly hear is that of constant performance at the expense of our humanness. Gentle power invites us to land into our heart as we power on.

The Finnish concept of sisu also plays a major role in this book. *Sisu* doesn't have a close synonym in any language, but the term denotes a kind of extraordinary inner strength in the face of adversity and is about not giving up, no matter what you're up against. Rooting back hundreds of years, sisu has been a well-kept secret—a way of life and philosophy that has impacted generations of Finns. It's not that we intended to keep it to ourselves. It's just that sisu is like the air we breathe or the way one has learned to tie their shoelaces—most of the time we don't even think of it, and so we don't talk about it. Although many Finns would be eager to describe sisu through their personal stories, for most of the word's history, sisu has been elusive and poorly understood. It's a unique construct that's easier to give examples of than define. Sisu is most often illustrated when we face the slimmest of odds and must reach beyond our known capacities. We arrive at the edge of our preconceived mental or physical limits to find, almost by magic, a previously unexpressed reserve of energy that carries us forward to the next moment. If you've endured significant adversity, reached for a goal far greater than your assumed capacities, or pushed through ominous challenges you had no idea how you'd complete, you've experienced sisu.

Sisu as a term made its grand appearance on the global stage during WWII when the comparably tinier Finnish military, against all possible odds, resisted the mammoth-sized invading Soviet Army. In Finland, the battle, fought over the course of 108 days amidst the harshest winter recorded at that time, is still referred to as the "Miracle of Winter War." The *New York Times* headline from January 14, 1940 read: "Sisu: A Word That Explains Finland,"[1] but afterward, sisu returned to obscurity other than among Finns and aficionados of long-distance running, who knew all about the epic history of Finnish endurance running.

While being a culture or a way life, at the same time sisu is deeply personal and is known as that which will enable the individual to cut "even through a stone wall."[2] Whether a literal stone barrier or one of the many proverbial walls of fear, shame, or doubt, we all share an inner beauty and power that enables us to break through, keep moving forward no matter what, voice our truths despite our fear of repercussions, and take big chances against small odds.

Even though I'm Finnish by birth, my path to researching sisu as a psychological construct has felt accidental. My work has its origin in a personal journey through violent trauma that occurred about twelve years ago. I had just moved to New York City with my then boyfriend of six months. Soon after, the relationship took a tragic turn into deepening emotional control and manipulation and, ultimately, physical violence. In the end, my former partner was convicted and deported from the United States. The warning signs had been there all along: the gaslighting, his planting seeds of doubt regarding my personal and professional competence, the sometimes-dizzying emotional intensity, and his push to move our relationship forward quickly. He was playing to my codependency and lack of self-worth at the time (I don't think I even knew the terms codependency and self-worth back then), and I hadn't yet learned how to say *no* when it's the only sane thing to do. He also took advantage of my undying faith in the goodness of all people. When it came to gentle power, I certainly erred on the soft end of the continuum—I truly believed it was my ill-fated duty to nurse him into healing and emotional wholeness.

Finding my way out of that abusive trance, I recounted the decisions that led me to such a relationship in the first place. In the process, I started wondering about personal power and self-leadership and their role in helping humans more generally overcome extreme adversity. These questions ultimately led me back to my home country and to sisu, which in its positive expression could be reasoned to contribute to Finland consistently rating at the top of happiest and least corrupt countries in the world. Sisu and integrity go hand in hand, and Finns are known for doing their best even when no one is looking. In fact, some years ago, *Reader's Digest* performed a "lost wallet test" in which reporters misplaced wallets in different cities around the world.[3] The wallets contained $50 with contact information, family photos, and business cards. Eleven out of every twelve wallets dropped in the Finnish capital of Helsinki were returned to their owners, making it the most "honest" city of the lost wallet test.

> Sisu is more than just fortitude—it's an entire
> way of thinking, leading, and engaging with life.

Thanks in part to recent attention to Nordic lifestyle in general and concepts like *hygge* (the Danish concept of coziness and contentment) and *lagom* (the Swedish term for "just right" or "life balance"), sisu has gained more traction on the global stage. Unfortunately, I too often see sisu reduced in the mainstream media to a kind of cultural essentialism regarding certain Finnish traits and markers. Sisu isn't just about long-distance running, ice swimming, stubbornness, or staying way too long in a hot sauna. It's even more than the magic of mental toughness and perseverance that most personal development books today promise as the Holy Grail of success.

Although sisu doesn't have a close counterpart in other languages, there are a handful of cultural cousins related to unearthing something exquisite within oneself when a lot is at stake: *ganbaru* and *gaman* in Japanese, *chutzpah* in Yiddish and Hebrew, *l'chatchila ariber* in Yiddish, and *rasmia* in Spanish among them. A notable difference about sisu is that it specifically refers to something embodied (sisu literally means "guts," "the inside," or "the intestines"). While you might not be able to *see* sisu, its impact in a time of trouble is visible, and it's pretty irreplaceable in the business of thriving and staying alive. But sisu is even more than that—it's an entire way of thinking, leading, and engaging with life that involves deep-seated qualities like integrity, honesty, discernment, and sovereignty.

At its best, sisu is what I'm calling gentle power—a harmonious and helpful approach to life itself, specifically in how we make decisions, relate to one another, and view ourselves both in times of crisis and peace. But sisu also has a shadow side, and when expressed, it can prevent us from evolving and succeeding in life. My work on sisu and gentle power is all about using sisu in positive ways to shape leaders, cultures, and human lives for the better. To this end, gentle power isn't just a call to embrace the "soft skills" of empathetic listening, nonviolent communication, and efficient problem solving. Gentle power is more nuanced than skill-building; it means becoming conscious of our values, patterns, behaviors, and effects on the world around us and allowing this awareness to materialize as better action. Gentle power is an internal shift—an alchemical integration of our strong and supple polarities. This process is intimate and personal, but it's also communal and universal.

This book is for anyone curious about embracing more of their full potential as a human. To truly benefit from it, you must be ready to undertake a journey within and begin your own initiatory quest into new frontiers. The good news is that you don't have to run across New Zealand to do that (not all of us have to run thousands of miles due to their unusually thick head like I did). As I learned the hard way, less is often more, and there's no inherent glory in constant hardship and self-sacrifice. It's my sincere hope that your own path to gentle power involves more gentleness—both regarding your own challenges and those of others—and that whatever difficulties you encounter along the way are meaningful and beneficial in the end. Having said that, no matter what form your journey takes, you must actively bring your own ideas and inquiries into daily practice. Without that, this book won't help much.

I also wrote this book to share my conviction that leadership is more about awareness and discernment than we've been told. Through the lens of sisu and gentle power, leadership is about uncovering our deep-seated potential for grace and offering the fruits of our resolute inner work to the world. Leadership manifests in all of us in our everyday lives; it isn't just the purview of jet-setting influencers or individuals who happen to be decorated for political, athletic, or entrepreneurial feats. All of us are called to a personal reckoning with power and leadership as we explore our natural potentiality.

In the following chapters, I invite you to journey with me across the rich landscape of self-inquiry by examining the concepts of gentleness and inner strength that unite to build the foundation of how we think, lead, succeed, and show up in the world. Leadership is action with impact. Our success as leaders depends on the kind of world we create through those actions. Our exploration, therefore, includes finding harmony between fortitude and gentleness, and it concludes with an invitation to recognize and develop gentle power through daily practice (*sadhana*). There are some contemplative prompts in the book, but especially in Chapter 14, to support your journey. I would even encourage getting a special notebook to answer these questions and document your gentle power journey. But first we must prepare for our voyage. To that end, part 1 of this book unpacks the concepts of leadership and power and how they play out with our peers, family members, and communities.

I hope that by exploring the ideas in this book, you'll begin to recognize the central and life-giving role of power and gentleness in your life and in your interactions with others and begin to manifest more peace and harmony in your life. *May you discover your own practice to effortlessly integrate gentle power into your daily existence.*

Welcome to the journey! Let's get started.

PART I

Opening Thoughts on Leadership and Power

CHAPTER 1:

You Are the Leader Now

We change the world not by what we say or do but as a consequence of what we have become. . . . The great become legendary when they teach by example. It isn't what they have, nor what they do, but what they have become that inspires all of mankind.

–DAVID HAWKINS[1]

My gaze was glued to the fourteen tiny windows on the screen in front of me, each window a portal to a lifetime of experience, wisdom, intelligence, and sisu—all hallmarks of the trials and triumphs characteristic of human life. My classmates were all suspended before me in the digital canvas of my Zoom app, and I listened closely as one shared her thoughts on conscious parenting and witnessed how she beamed over her success in connecting more deeply with her two children due to the inner work she had committed to doing with herself.

This was in May 2021, and I was attending the online closing ceremony of an Authentic Relating Training (AR) leadership training course organized by Authentic Relating Training International, whose mission is to offer people foundational tools to build emotional intimacy, authentic relating, trust, and profound connection in everyday life. AR courses usually happen in person during weekend or week-long retreats, but the pandemic—like most other things at the time—put a damper on all of that. And so my classmates and I met online to learn and apply the AR method, beginning with five simple yet potentially life-revolutionizing approaches to leadership, which are:

- Welcome everything with authentic curiosity.
- Assume nothing when relating and communicating with others.

- Reveal your experience instead of concealing it.
- Own your experience, instead of blaming yourself or others.
- Honor yourself and others.

During the AR course, our group must have gone through a decade's worth of leadership moments that asked (and sometimes forced) us to take what we had learned in class and apply it to real life. Some used their authentic-relating skills to navigate the end of partnerships in a more conscious and connected way. One of my classmates used what they learned to leave the job they had for decades to follow their passion for music. Another was able to build more meaningful interactions with their parents and siblings. And several of us, perhaps for the very first time, learned to recognize and express our authentic *yeses* and *nos* instead of following lifelong habits of people-pleasing, codependency, and control to ensure acceptance and safety.

What struck me most at the closing ceremony was that none of us were what you would traditionally call *leaders*. We weren't big-time CEOs, founders, or executives. We were teachers, small business owners, parents, researchers, alternative medicine practitioners, and consultants with a shared desire for self-knowledge and deeper connection in relationships. In that moment, sitting in my living room with those fourteen little windows on my screen, I experienced a beautiful reminder of what true leadership can look like. Each of us was committed, courageous, and ready to show up for ourselves and each other. Far from grand gestures, noble words, and public acclaim, leadership often remains uncelebrated and unrecognized. More often than not, leadership is the everyday pursuit of integrity, grace, and betterment of the human condition.

Each of us in the AR program was a tiny, unassuming ode to the pursuit of truth and genuine expression. Nobody else on the Zoom call knew it, but I was suddenly overcome with a profound wave of hope that makes my heart light up just remembering it. If *we* could do this—if we could know ourselves and communicate better in lives packed with work, parenting, money concerns, ailing relatives, and relationship struggles— then this is was a proof of concept that anyone could.

Leading others is first and foremost about leading ourselves. Leadership requires that we become intimately informed about our beliefs, habits, and relationship to power. It's about recognizing our patterns of self-importance, our need for control, and the ways in which we might disconnect emotionally. And leadership is also about doing whatever inner work it takes to establish self-worth, maintain healthy boundaries, and embody our sovereignty. Of course, the path of personal leadership can feel overwhelming at times and quite often as if we're alternating between one step forward and two steps back. There have been times when I've felt frustrated out of my skull with my tendency to stumble into the same potholes of my character and when all I wanted was to do was hide away in a remote cave for the foreseeable future until I either became enlightened or simply passed.

Thankfully, it doesn't always feel like that. And we're certainly not the first people stumbling toward greater understanding and personal growth. This is a journey traversed by people of all walks of life across millennia, and it hasn't been just monks and philosophers and mystics but ordinary people like you and me. In a way, it's the oldest and most important journey we can take because it's the only one that can connect us with our heart, reconnect us to others, and ultimately reconcile the human family. I'm referring to the "examined life" that Socrates encouraged us to pursue (ironically during the trial in which he was sentenced to death). On this journey, our progress isn't measured in kilometers or miles or in units of time, but in the lessons we learn along the way.

Regardless of our profession, age, or social status, our paths invariably run through the crucible, or *dojo*, of everyday life. By definition, a dojo, which is a Japanese word, is "the place of the way," and although the word typically refers to a training hall where martial arts are practiced, in this case, our dojo is our entire life. It is everything we encounter. In this training hall, we can use any experience as a training tool or partner—everything and everyone we encounter is an invitation to learn, grow, and test our skills as we refine the vocabulary of our hearts to become better at relating to ourselves and others. Every moment offers us two options—to evolve and connect or to contract, control, and close ourselves off. Ideally, we choose the first, but whatever option we engage the most over time determines how we experience the world.

Although they were thousands of miles away from me, I could *feel* my AR classmates because they chose to practice an expansive and open style of leadership. That's what genuine leadership is like—it is personal and therefore authentic, and because it is authentic, it is felt in the body as trust or something inherently life-giving that is expanding.

When it comes to leadership, it's not like we're dealing with a lack of information or interest in the subject. Just search for "leadership" on Google or Amazon and try to make sense of the thousands of results. Our problem isn't supply but application. We need to make use of what we already know, and to do that, we need to focus on what matters most and ask the right questions. On that topic, I've included lots of information in this book and probably way more information than is possible to absorb in a single reading. Instead of trying to learn or apply everything here, I suggest finding just two or three pieces that resonate with you most and applying them as a daily practice (more about creating your *sadhana* toward the end of the book). The path to self-leadership is best traveled with small, mindful steps.

Throughout this journey, please remember that leadership is an inherent quality in every one of us. Leaders aren't just executives, political or spiritual figures, and social influencers; leaders are all of us, no matter our station or walk of life. All of us are potent agents within the multitude of social systems we are part of, and each of us holds the power to create, change, and elevate our individual and collective realities.

My deadline to finish the manuscript for this book coincided with my fortieth birthday and the completion of my doctoral dissertation. On top of all that, I'd been experiencing an inner imperative to review my entire life to decide what to leave behind and what habits, goals, and relationships I wanted to bring into the new decade. I was overwhelmed, to say the least. Fortunately, I was lucky enough to organize a thirty-day solo getaway to a tiny fishing village on the northeast coast of Bali. The plan was to finish my outstanding projects, review my life, and welcome more balance into my gentle power equation.

It's impossible for us not to influence the world through our presence—and leadership.

Water has always been my element, but in the past, I was never all that eager to actually submerge myself in it. I used to much rather observe the deep blue from a distance than get wet. However, on the wings of my impending midlife transition, things changed, and I decided to go swimming in the ocean every day while I was there. One morning while I was in the ocean, I observed some colorful little fish nuzzling the ocean floor beneath my shadow. I must have appeared to them like a giant spaceship with bubbles coming out of it. What had once been a thriving coral paradise was gone (an unfortunate reality for marine life in many places on our planet), and it now resembled a warzone or the scorched landscape after a forest fire. As the fish wandered nonchalantly around their destroyed seascape, I thought to myself how they have no clue that there once had been a beautiful reef, that they most likely don't even comprehend they're in water. Those fish live and swim and nuzzle their entire lives in that environment. It's their reality; it's all they know. And it occurred to me that we humans are not so different. We spend our whole lives surrounded by a particular mindset and collection of stories about the world, and we keep repeating them to ourselves and others, rarely questioning them, and even more rarely knowing that they're even there.

As far as I know, the difference between us and those fish is that we can consciously analyze and introspect our reality and the environments we belong to. The beliefs we hold about ourselves, our past, and our future can change over time, which means that how we perceive reality changes too. Although traditional psychology has been informed by an idea that we're mainly pushed by the past, as our experiences, traumas, and subconscious programming act as the blueprint for our action, I once heard Martin Seligman (the founder of positive psychology) say that we are "pulled by the future." He went on to share that the human mind scans everything it experiences in the now to create simulations of future scenarios. I later found out that our brains do so with a subconscious processing power of roughly eight to eleven million kilobytes per second of information, whereas conscious processing operates at around fifty kilobytes per second.[2] This subconscious processing that is automatic, unconscious, and instant is called System 1 by Nobel Laureate Daniel Kahneman, and it involves our emotions, the blueprint of our culture, past experiences, beliefs, and also our expectations. When we switch to what Kahneman further calls System 2, which is a more deliberate and rational processing of information, we can slow down enough to consciously think about our choices and thus, lead ourselves. We can choose the future we wished to be pulled by—as leaders, it is crucial we do this part well.

Gaining mastery in anything, let alone our thinking, takes commitment over a long period of time, but all positive changes begin with the first step. Even choosing to read a book on gentle power is a great start. Hopefully, it's enough to inspire the first step on your journey toward something deeply transformative.

The Magic of Everyday Leadership

According to Yuval Noah Harari, a professor of history at the Hebrew University in Jerusalem, despite all the challenges we face in the world today, the most crucial struggle of our time is a lack of leadership.[3] Harari rose to global recognition with his bestselling books *Sapiens* and *Homo Deus*, in which he describes in plain language the past, present, and near future of our species. As a historian, he examines our past decision-making as humans as well as our patterns of behavior to illuminate potential paths for our future. If we lack good leadership in all of this, it's an undeniable problem.

Leadership can be viewed as actions infused with the intention to help people become empowered themselves. This creates even more resources and opportunities for them, which in turn encourages more action rooted in what I'm calling gentle power—the balanced expression of our strength and care. Although daily moments at the office or at home with our family can feel mundane, I like to see them as portals of micro-leadership. Each moment we are challenged and choose to remain open to learning and reflecting, we give birth to a better reality with our colleagues, spouse, children, friends, and anyone else we come in contact with. Like Jason Digges—a cofounder of the ART International—shares in his book *Conflict = Energy: The Transformative Practice of Authentic Relating*, every moment like that is an opportunity to alchemize conflict into clarity and therefore, gain greater awareness about ourselves and others.[4] Self-leadership is the path of growth, of openness, and of using our sisu to shine light upon our shadow. Every time someone makes the decision to contemplate their choices and use everyday challenges for transformation and growth, they are being a leader by using their power to grow, take responsibility, and influence their reality for the better.

About five years ago, while I was rushing to get everything prepped for a Sisu Not Silence event in Helsinki, I was having a lunch meeting with a friend who was helping me with the event. I don't quite remember what was going on, but it felt like he was being indecisive, and there were assignments that had been lagging for days. I felt frustrated and stressed as the pressure of our deadlines drew nearer. As I stood up to close our meeting, I said, "Thank you so much for the lunch. I've got to get back to doing our work now." And then I added, somewhat underhandedly, "Since it's clearly not going to finish itself."

My friend responded with a hesitant look. My comment and delivery conveyed a lot of the judgment I was feeling against him, and in my heart, I knew it. Ironically, I was in the middle of writing an article about compassion and leadership. The yucky feelings of the exchange wouldn't leave me alone. Knowing I could do better, I took an honest look at myself and reviewed the judgments and projections I'd been putting on him for some time. I apologized to him for what I'd said and told him I knew I could do better than airing my subconscious laundry like that. He smiled and said, "Yeah, that felt a bit *unironed*, but I know you've been under a lot of stress, and I know I could've been more on it with a couple of these assignments." Then he thanked me for being open and for reflecting on my actions. "I appreciate your effort to put growth before pride," he added.

To paraphrase from a few pages back, the Authentic Relating program has since taught me to question my assumptions when communicating with others, to welcome whatever happens with curiosity, to talk about my experience instead of masking it, to take responsibility, and to do my best to honor myself and others. Ideally, that's what the leadership I want to embody looks like. On the other hand, doing the opposite of authentic relating: holding tightly to preconceived notions about others, keeping up defensive barriers when none are called for, hiding my true feelings in order to control situations and other people, projecting my own insecurities and mistakes on them, and treating others and myself with little respect are a recipe for distrust and a lack of connection and intimacy. Gentle power includes several facets, and one of them is open and compassionate communication rooted in taking personal responsibility. Doing so helps us mine challenging situations and inevitable conflicts with others for the gold of true intimacy.

Gentle power requires that we assume the responsibilities of leadership. Leaders aren't far-away mythical figures like unicorns; they're us. If we think that leadership is something that mostly happens outside of ourselves, it's all too easy to run from our own shadows and triggers, and our potential for growth is severely diminished. But when I'm able to look into the mirror without excessive emotionality and own up to my part in the dynamic, things start moving. The moment with my friend described above could have easily led to more misunderstanding and disconnection, but my commitment to examine my behaviors and his willingness to be patient with my incomplete yet sincere efforts to grow as a leader led to a deepening in our connection.

Sisu isn't about some superhuman resolve; it's about holding ourselves to a self-chosen set of standards. Sisu involves a sense of *inner authority*—a fantastic concept I learned from Rick Smith, a senior course leader in the Authentic Relating Training International. Inner authority is about refining ourselves in each moment and welcoming personal power inside our own skin. It's about having the courage to welcome anything that wants our attention. As defined by Rick, inner authority isn't a tight, vigilant, hard-edged endeavor—it's simply about being an author of what's happening with us and embracing the sometimes-uncomfortable charge inherent to being in charge. Inner authority is where healthy charisma and inspiration come from in leadership. It also aligns with what Harari is calling our world leaders to manifest with urgency. Without inner authority and the intimate process of personal leadership it entails, self-awareness, critical thinking, and collaboration are unlikely.

Like leadership itself, inner authority is available to all of us. Each of us has what it takes, and realizing that is the first step to an adventure of a lifetime. Just like the example of my Authentic Relating classmates I opened the chapter with, all it takes for us to shift our environment are deliberate and daily acts toward inner growth by taking advantage of the portals to micro-leadership presented to us in everyday life. The more we do this work as individuals, the more impact it has on all of us.

Leadership, power, success, and influence . . . we need to reexamine all these terms, reimagine what they could mean for us, and reprogram ourselves accordingly. And if there ever was a time to do so, right now is the moment to get jiggy with it.

CHAPTER 2:

Getting Over the Power Paralysis

*The fundamental concept in social science is power, in
the same sense in which energy is the fundamental
concept in physics. . . . The laws of social dynamics are
laws which can only be stated in terms of power.*

–BERTRAND RUSSELL[1]

A fter a friend of mine read part of the early draft of this book, she came to me looking profoundly concerned. "Leadership is such a key topic," she said, "and I'm glad you approach sisu from that particular angle. But it makes me uncomfortable that you have to make it so much about power. After all, don't you think that what the world needs is more compassion and kindness?"

It's a valid question. And my friend is by no means alone in her apprehension when it comes to that loaded word: *power*. I know; I've struggled with it too. Power has been such a charged issue for most of my life. As someone who's overcome domestic violence, I've experienced the damaging side of power firsthand. Because I suffered from that kind of abuse in my intimate relationship, I wanted to make sure nobody would feel unsafe in my presence. I acquired a subconscious habit to hold my body in a particular way in social situations to express my undivided attention to others and their needs. I did this by tilting my head slightly sideways and downward to show that I was friendly and nonthreatening. In a world with so much hatred and abuse of power, this type of behavior is understandable. Unfortunately, when rooted in fear rather than healthy self-worth, it doesn't ultimately help build the healthy relationships we all need.

I want to start this chapter by distinguishing healthy relationships from those I have labeled *entanglements*. Entanglements here have nothing to do with the wondrous phenomenon of quantum physics in which two particles separated by large distance experience an intimately linked and shared state. In fact, its quite the opposite. Entanglements as I use the term in this context are called that because they're not so much relationships as they are entwined interpersonal bundles of fears, triggers, and unconscious patterns. Entanglements are characterized by unspoken contracts in which two or more parties in the exchange dance around each other's wounds and ego-needs at the expense of truth, genuine connection, growth, and sovereignty.

All our behaviors (my agreeable head-tilting, for example) and preferences for certain behaviors in others (to look for agreeable head-tilters) originate in our basic needs for safety and acceptance, as well as from our past attempts to meet those fundamental needs. I'll get into this topic more in part 4 of the book, but for now I want to examine how it relates to power, especially our preconceived ideas about power.

When it comes to developing gentle power (which I sometimes refer to as *graceful strength*), there's no one-size-fits-all approach. Although we share many of the same basic needs, our experiences of meeting those needs—either successfully or otherwise—are quite different. That means that some of us might need to lean into the tougher side of the equation, while others of us should focus more on cultivating compassion, softness, and gentleness. Wherever you are on the continuum, I wrote this book to help you reach greater clarity and empowerment.

The Courage to Exceed Ourselves

Take a quick look at mainstream news or social media and you'll invariably come across images and stories characterized by fear, victimhood, and powerlessness. I'm not talking about the millions of people around the planet who have been truly wronged in some way and have plenty to be afraid of; I'm talking about the contemporary culture of disempowerment. Not to be overly judgmental here, but it sometimes seems like most of us are doing it, particularly people who have little reason to consider themselves disempowered. Once an idea starts to make the rounds, it's rare that people question it.

Take aging, for example. For the longest time—especially in the West—middle-age and beyond have been almost synonymous with all sorts of unwanted marks of physical decline: reduced strength, increased body fat, reduced bone density, and loss of libido. Even though the latest research in longevity and physical thriving into our later years says otherwise, some people still take it for granted that you're done for after your pass the midway point in life. It's the same thing with personal agency and self-leadership. If we don't believe that we can influence our own thinking and affect the world around us, it might as well be true.

Abraham Maslow was the founder of humanistic psychology and is widely considered to be one of the most influential psychologists ever. His work on the hierarchy of needs and self-actualization has influenced generations of thinkers, but Maslow's emphasis on leadership tends to be lesser known. For example, he strongly encouraged his students to treat themselves and each other as if they were world leaders.[2] Maslow recognized that this was difficult for most of us. We have an inherent fear of grandiosity and pride, almost as if we were afraid of being punished for it, like Adam or Prometheus were for imagining themselves as godlike. According to Maslow, we associate thinking too highly of ourselves with loss, scarcity, and exile. As we say in Finland (again, the country rated as happiest in the world), "Too much joy inevitably leads to tears."

Maslow invited his students to seek to be even more godlike than they already were. He implored them not to renounce "heroism, your own nobility, your own highest potentialities—with humility as a defense."[3] His encouragement is even more notable when you consider that Maslow's parents were Jewish immigrants who came to America to flee persecution in the early twentieth century. People of Maslow's generation had seen far too much of political figures—namely, Stalin and Hitler—who had considered themselves as godlike and caused untold suffering to millions on account of it. Individuals who'd lived through WWII knew the dangers of thinking too much of themselves.

Like climate disruption, power and the misuse of power exist whether we recognize it or not.

Even so, Maslow insisted that it was a mistake to fall into the trap of "castrating ourselves, by making ourselves too small, too humble, too meek, too mild—renouncing ambition, renouncing high goals, renouncing high aspirations and saying: 'You don't have to be afraid of me. I'm no challenge to anybody. Poor little me; I'm no threat.'"[4] It's not lost on me that this sounds a lot like the head-tilting I referenced a few pages back. Maslow also pointed out that one could be proud and godlike while still expressing humility and that it was the lack of humility that led to paranoia and abuse in leaders. In the same way, the vision of gentle power I'm presenting here requires both gentleness and power.

If we're not familiar with our discomfort around power, we simply can't be strong and balanced leaders. What we resist will persist. That which is left unexamined in the unconscious is where our shadow and the unhealed parts of our psyche lie. Do I trust myself enough to use power, or do I feel I cannot be trusted with it? Will I too end up creating harm and perpetuating hurt like my parents or the leaders I witness in the world today? Like climate disruption, power and the misuse of power exist whether we recognize it or not. Turning away and ignoring the issue does nothing to stop the disaster.

In order for us to foster gentle power, it's important to understand what power means to us, how we resist it, and how we may have abused our power in the past. It may also involve looking into where we entertain patterns of inferiority so that we don't even have to look at what our actual relationship to power is as well as where we avoid doing the inner work it takes to rise to our full potential. Gentle power is an invitation to a wild, raw, rewarding, and authentic journey into leadership, and it calls us to look at everything about our lives—our trauma triggers, our current relationships, aversions, and affections, and the attachment wounds and patterns formed in childhood.

How Power Works

Eric Liu is an American teacher and civics practitioner whose TED-Ed talk "Why Ordinary People Need to Understand Power" has over two million views. Liu says that although people have a lot of triggers around the concept and practice of power and that they sometimes consider power to be detrimental or evil, it nevertheless is a neutral force. Just like fire or physics, power is neither good nor bad. Liu is an avid proponent of civics because he sees it as the canvas for the elevating use of power. Civics, as Liu defines it, "is the art of citizenship. [It] is the art of being a pro-social problem-solver, and it is about showing up for life. It encompasses a foundation of values, an understanding of the systems that make the world go round, and a set of skills that allow you to pursue goals and to have others join in that pursuit."[5] At its core, civics prizes personal leadership and our ability to make a difference through our choices, and it all begins with demystifying power, understanding how it works, and ultimately learning how to use it.

Liu describes six types of power:

- physical force
- wealth
- state action
- social norms
- numbers
- ideas

In short, *physical force* is power at its most primal. It's based on control and imposing fear onto others. *Wealth* provides the ability to influence outcomes and purchase almost any of the other kinds of power listed here. *State action* is organized compulsion on a larger scale, and *social norms* include all the unwritten rules regarding behaviors and beliefs in a given society. The power of *numbers* simply describes the ways in which people can unite to create the critical mass needed for change. Finally, *ideas* drive everything around us. Every great deed and legacy was once an idea that gave birth to inspired action.

Liu notes that power is disproportionately distributed, and the small group of people who understand how power works is all too happy to wield it, especially over those who are encouraged to remain disengaged or willfully ignorant. Rye Barcott writes, "talent is universal, but opportunity is not."[6] In a similar way, while everyone has power and choice, it's important to acknowledge that they are proportional to one's social privilege. While gentle power requires that we devote ourselves to inner work, it also calls for us to enact the social changes necessary to enable others to do the same.

Power in Relationships

Even when we're not aware of it, power plays a significant role in our interpersonal relationships. Studies support the commonsense notion that the partner with more power in a romantic relationship usually dominates conversations and has more to say on decisions important to the relationship.[7] As I'll discuss later in the book, powerlessness in relationships is associated with domestic violence, abuse in its various forms, and diminished mental health.

If you recognize the signs of abuse in your own relationship, regardless of whether you are the recipient of it or the abuser, I urge you to seek help from a local domestic violence support organization. Most of them provide services to victims and overcomers, and increasingly more are offering support to those who commit and perpetrate abusive patterns. Remember that abuse doesn't simply refer to physical violence. Emotional abuse and psychological manipulation are extremely damaging as well, if only because they tend to be more covert (and therefore can take much longer to recognize and act upon).

The dyadic power-social influence model (DPSIM) is helpful in describing how power operates specifically within close relationships.[8] These relationships are distinctly unlike those we might temporarily share with strangers or the structured and hierarchical relationships we're in at work. Particularly when close relationships are voluntary, power and the tactics we employ to influence the relationship must be used in appropriate and judicious ways in order for the relationship to remain balanced. The DPSIM borrows select constructs and principles from several power theories to create four sets of constructs that are critical to understanding the operation of power and influence within relationships:

- The characteristics of the involved partners (attractiveness, warmth, reliability, status, wealth, attachment orientation, personality traits, and so on)

- The types of power each partner has access to (reward, coerciveness, legitimacy, expertise, reference, and information)[9]
- The styles of influence and strategies each might deploy (direct versus indirect, for example)
- The outcomes that members of the relationship experience as a result of their behavior and power (such as well-being, trust, commitment, depression, anxiety)

The matrix of each relationship is determined by the myriad configurations and reconfigurations of these variables over time.

The creators of the DPSIM note that power is also a matter of perception. We very well may not recognize our actual power or power resources (either ours or those of our partner), and we can learn to tap into these for greater influence and relational harmony. For example, partners regularly have different areas of expertise or access to information. Acknowledging these differences and working with them can prove quite beneficial for both sides of the relationship.

The creators of the DPSIM also note that power is more than persuasive influence but is also the ability to resist influence as well. We can't always control what happens around us—how other people behave, for example, or the effects of market forces, politics, and social media. We can, however, exercise our power through our discernment, by making informed decisions and choosing when to enact our power when it counts the most. This is why I continually emphasize the importance of self-understanding and awareness. It isn't only a matter of learning how to better empower ourselves but also knowing the areas in which we tend to give power away (and overuse power as well). Influence is rooted in our awareness of the dynamics of power in our relationships, in all the many ways that power manifests between and among people. The better we understand this, the more informed our decisions become across all domains of life.

Reexamining Our Beliefs

For the longest time growing up, I had this story about myself that I was bad at running and that running simply wasn't for me. That all changed one August morning in my hometown of Seinäjoki. The day was so delightful and crisp that a brief jog turned into a full forty minutes of running, which was a big deal for me. If you would've told me then that thirteen years later, I'd start training to run across New Zealand, I would've been shocked out of my sneakers. I also had a story about myself that said I was the type of person who would never tolerate domestic abuse, but that didn't hold true either.

It takes reviewing the beliefs we hold about ourselves to notice any limiting, diminishing, or erroneous storylines that influence our decision-making and affect our quality of life. Conversely, it takes self-awareness and self-examination to detect those parts of ourselves that are working beautifully and cultivate them even more. Reviewing our patterns of thinking is one potent way to access more power because our ideas and thoughts have so much say about our experience of reality.

The Price of Powerlessness

Whereas the ability to exercise control over our lives leads to a greater sense of security, autonomy, and well-being (and having more capacity to help others), the inability to do so leads to a sense of powerlessness. According to Dacher Keltner, after climate disruption, powerlessness is the greatest threat to humanity.[10]

Keltner is a professor of social psychology at UC Berkeley in California who has researched the topic of power for the past twenty-five years to understand how it influences our lives. He stresses that powerlessness amplifies our sensitivity to threat and pushes us into the neurological states most associated with protection and survival. Unfortunately, these states limit our capacity to make informed decisions, act consciously, express our creativity, feel happiness and a sense of meaning, and enjoy good mental health. Most of us have experienced these effects in one way or the other, and they're far too common in our work life. A sense of limited resources, for example, drives people to remain in jobs that are outright exploitative. Even executives—while seemingly enjoying greater power due to their hierarchical position—are often operating from a sense of powerlessness.

Powerlessness typically manifests in the sense that life is something that is happening to you or happening at a speed you can't control. It can feel like you're always a few steps behind and that most of your time is spent putting out fires and getting nowhere. It's far too easy to get caught in the cycle of powerlessness, and it takes waking up to your own agency and autonomy to jump off. Unfortunately, powerlessness also encourages mental and physical lethargy. This is why society is currently relying upon so much outsourcing in politics, health care, and the consumer market.

> Manifesting power means that we make
> our decisions from courage, completeness
> and a sense of healthy self-worth.

That being said, the tide is often moving against us. The systems we find ourselves in are often so complex that the sheer amount of information we need just to make informed decisions encourages powerlessness in all of us (not to mention that some of the crucial information we need is regularly hidden from us). And how are we supposed to overcome our experience of powerlessness when we're juggling the demands of work, parenthood, bills, health crises, and so on? Most of us outsource our power to simply catch our breath, but the systems that exercise power—the systems we then become more reliant upon—take this into account and reward us accordingly. Before we know it, more of our lives feel out of our control. This is one way in which we remove ourselves from the council of power and habitually disengage from being active partici-pants in creating a world that is a safe, abundant, and just place to live in. This dynamic is the same regardless of whether we're talking about politics, health decisions, or intimate relationships.

Powerlessness leads to the illusion that resources are way scarcer than they actually are. We can be blind to the opportunities in front of us and view other people as inherently selfish or out to get us. When we're stressed and depleted, still healing from past trauma, or haven't yet acknowledged the legacy of past wounds, it's way easier to feel like the underdog in life. We take on a mindset of just being grateful for what little we are given in life, even though it's not often what we want or it leaves us unfulfilled. This is what William James—the philosopher and "father" of modern psychology—referred to as the "habit of inferiority."[11]

On the other hand, manifesting power means that we make our decisions from wholeness, courage, completeness, and want, instead of from lack, scarcity, fear, or need. As Maslow stressed, it is far too easy to live small and consider ourselves (and others) as inferior, which is perhaps why Maslow is so well-known for his work on self-actualization, which is essentially the optimization of personal power. Acting with power means that our self-worth is firmly in place. It means that we don't negotiate our place in life or bargain our values out of fear that we'll be punished if we say *no*.

I recently coached a client who wanted to find a loving partner and start a family. Her struggle was that while she was very conscious and deeply committed to her inner work, she was also still healing from the trauma of being with an alcoholic partner for a decade. On one of our phone sessions, she told me that she was dating someone new and had noticed some red flags around his lack of communication and emotional unavailability. Most people expect the other party in a relationship to be equally present, but my client was doubting herself by questioning the validity of her boundaries and whether a partner even needs to be emotionally available. "Maybe it's just that he's busy and I'm being overly sensitive," she said. While that could be the case in some other instance, because my client's boundaries weren't yet firm enough to keep her empowered and she was only working to establish her self-worth, I sensed that she might be at risk for yet another entanglement—and to bargain on her principle of feeling emotionally met.

Keltner asserts that powerlessness is a primary contributor to most of our psychological and medical struggles because it has such a big physiological impact on our body. When our body is constantly on the defensive and suffering from stress, our ability to weigh our options and think creatively is impaired. Furthermore, increased stress can mean more depression, headaches, back pain, chronic inflammation, high blood pressure, lowered immunity, and other physical struggles that enhance our sense of powerlessness even more.[12] Repeated exposure can even lead to post-traumatic stress disorder (PTSD).

According to Keltner, it is virtually impossible to succeed or gain the security and love we need when we are feeling powerless. Powerlessness impairs our discernment, and we can easily make life decisions from that state that come with regrettable consequences. A sense of power, on the other hand, helps us make the best choices for ourselves and others. Both power and powerlessness have strong emotional impacts. The client I was just writing about yearned to have a family of her own, but she felt disempowered in new relationships until she began to recognize her own role in creating that sense of powerlessness that left her feeling vulnerable, as if others were always holding the keys to the life she wanted. Fortunately, she gave the relationship above a pass and later found a partner who is emotionally present and committed to showing up for the development of their relationship.

When power is a dirty word in our lives, we tend to let it leak away. Why would we create healthy containers for something we feel disdain or mistrust of? But when we can understand better how power operates and how we can employ it as a force of good in the world, we can claim it with love and use it to shape our destiny. Whether you are in a time of refining your power or reclaiming the power you may have been giving away, doing so means entering a portal to a whole new you. You are the leader you have been waiting for.

Toxic Leadership

Even though we know more now about harmful leadership than ever before, people around the world still tolerate and follow these types of leaders even when they are clearly damaging in their influence and actions. According to some social scientists, there are four types of *dark leadership* or *dark charisma* that we normally lump into the category of toxic leadership that each have detrimental effects on organizations and other groups of people:[13]

- toxic
- destructive
- abusive
- ineffective

According to the researchers who make these distinctions, *toxic* leadership has a relatively low intent of harm and high ambiguity, which means that it goes more often unnoticed than the other three types. *Destructive* leadership, on the other hand, includes volitional behaviors and methods that outright contradict an organization's best interests and are harmful to its employees. *Abusive* leaders engage in sustained displays of verbal aggression and hostility (even physical), whereas *ineffective* leaders simply take a passive approach to their work.

Jean Lipman-Blumen was the first to research toxic leadership. Her work suggests that our brains are hardwired to respond to leaders who are best able to comfort our fears.[14] Our natural desire for safety and validation may lure us into tolerating poor leadership, especially when toxic leaders deliver results in some form. As John Paul Steele notes, there are "strong leaders who have the right stuff, but just in the wrong intensity, and with the wrong desired end-state, namely self-promotion above all else."[15]

The ethical standards, behavior, and integrity of those in power impact life quality and opportunities for billions of people around the world. Toxic leadership has the ability to destroy people, companies, and entire societies not only through creating confusion and ambiguity, but also because it impairs functioning and prevents people from doing their work in an optimal way. Toxic leaders, however, don't attain or maintain power by themselves, and recent research highlights the role of followers when it comes to toxic leaders remaining in power.[16] Followers are much more agential than previously believed, and they typically have all the power necessary to neutralize toxic leaders. According to this research, toxic leadership can lead to powerlessness and frustration among followers but can also result in situations in which followers abandon these leaders or take action to minimize their influence.

Power isn't taken; it's bestowed. Groups have the capacity to grant power to those who advance the greater good as well as the power to remove or undermine leaders who don't measure up to their standards (as the recent examples of the downfall of extremely powerful men like Jeffrey Epstein and Harvey Weinstein suggest). One of the key ideas of the Sisu Not Silence campaign is that bystanders are the fulcrum of change; they actually hold the keys to changing the ways in which we view and discuss abuse. It's the witnesses and bystanders due to their mass (power in numbers) who hold the keys to how perpetrators are seen and sanctioned in public dialogue as well as how survivors are viewed and treated (which should be with care and respect instead of disdain and doubt).

All too often we experience dark leadership right in front of our noses within our own families and relationships. I recently spoke with the bright teenage daughter of a friend whose deep brown eyes communicated incredible strength, but also immense sadness. "Dad's back home," she told me, "so we're all walking on eggshells again." This comment broke my heart. I know what it's like to have to be around someone whose mere presence diminishes your sense of safety, life energy, and well-being. The biggest journey a person experiencing abuse often makes is in reaching the point where the pain of tolerating someone's constant diminishing comments or other forms of abuse becomes greater than the pain of living with the situation. The perpetrator's power always grows in proportion to the victim's silence and powerlessness—in fact, the whole dynamic depends on it. In this sense, the bigger tragedy than the physical assaults I suffered was the fact that I believed my partner when he said that if I told anyone about the abuse, nobody would believe me or care. But he was wrong. When I finally spoke up, people did believe me, and the right people did care.

Keltner redefines power as "the capacity to make a difference in the world, in particular by stirring others in our social networks." This is in direct contrast to the Machiavellian view of power that equates it with force, fraud, and abuse, which Keltner indicates has negatively shaped our perceptions of power over the past several centuries. To the contrary, power is what "determines our empathy, generosity, civility, innovation, intellectual rigor, and the collaborative strength of our communities and social networks," Keltner continues.[17] Just like sisu, power is a paradox. It can allow us to make a difference in the world and enhance the lives of others, but it can also be wielded in manipulative, controlling, merciless, and harsh ways. How we handle this power paradox is what determines our quality of life individually, and it's also the key to the health of our larger society. Power always comes with a responsibility to nurture both our strength and our compassion.

PART II

Gentleness

CHAPTER 3:

Finding the Path

*What would you have? Your gentleness shall force
more than your force move us to gentleness.*

—SHAKESPEARE.[1]

S ince the first psychology class I took as an inquisitive seventeen
year old at Seinäjoki High School in the western part of Finland, I knew that to understand the human mind was my calling.
Even so, it took over a decade after saying goodbye to my hometown of
some twenty thousand people, a master's degree in social sciences, and
years of working abroad from New Delhi to New York for me to finally
reconnect with psychology. The transition came in the aftermath of a
career crisis that pushed me toward what I really want to do in life—
support people on their path to self-realization and empowerment. My
education in social psychology didn't really offer much of a profession,
but it taught me how to observe the world and ask good questions. So
that's what I did. "What makes me feel alive?" I asked myself. "How can
I fulfill my purpose? And what can I learn from others who have done
it before me?"

Positive Psychology

Even as a student, I'd never resonated with psychology's emphasis on
pathology—how it stresses the causes and effects of mental illness. In
2011, I hadn't yet heard of positive psychology, and it was a stroke of luck
that I happened to come across a book on the subject that someone had

misplaced in the fitness and bodybuilding section of the Barnes and Noble in Union Square. The book had a light-blue cover with a rather imposing yellow font: *Authentic Happiness: Using the New Positive Psychology to Realize Your Potential for Lasting Fulfillment* by Martin E. P. Seligman, PhD. By the end of the first chapter, I knew I'd found what I'd been looking for at that moment in my life.

Positive psychology focuses almost exclusively on well-being. It strives to understand what makes our lives worth living as well as the enabling factors that allow individuals to thrive.[2] Seligman coined the acronym PERMA to describe what people strive for in their pursuit of happiness:

- positive emotion
- engagement
- relationships
- meaning
- achievement

Instead of being viewed as a movement, positive psychology is best acknowledged for its contribution in focusing our attention and resources on the study of previously undervalued topics in psychology, such as hope, wisdom, creativity, courage, spirituality, responsibility, and perseverance.[3] Nobody lives only to be free of anxiety and illness, and a life well-lived consists of other elements than those involved in merely surviving and getting by. In direct contrast to most other approaches in the field of mental health, positive psychology is often called *the science of happiness*.

Positive psychology seeks to provide individuals, organizations, and communities the tools they need to thrive and flourish. Its aim isn't to replace or compete with mainstream psychology, but to broaden its focus beyond suffering and its alleviation.[4] Positive psychology focuses on how we can enhance well-being and identify what enables us to endure adversity and bounce back stronger than ever. To do this, this still-emerging field devotes research into the arenas of achievement, organizational development, creativity, and psychological health, and positive psychology has applications for everything from therapy, journalism, and education to sports, public health, and even law and governance.

The Long Road to Gentleness

One of the turning points in my run across New Zealand happened on the twelfth day of my fifty-day journey. I'd been running 30 miles each day, and I was nearing a total of 360 miles. My right ankle was swollen from the repeated pounding on the hard surface of the highway, and the heat raised the temperature of the road to 135°F, which traveled through the rubber soles of my shoes to my already-blistered feet, making them swell even more. I was in a great deal of pain, and things were getting tough. Mina Holder (my *crew queen*) is a British school teacher and ultrarunner herself who has run the famous Te Araroa Trail across New Zealand. Mina was commissioned as my trusted companion, coach, and unlicensed armchair psychologist during the run, while managing the practicalities of our day-to-day, and she had been very optimistic about my progress. However, I caught some worry on her face on that twelfth day. Mina had been taping my toes, preparing my meals, and driving the van that led a convoy of other people who'd joined us along the way by car, all of us slowly making our way up the western side of New Zealand.

Throughout the journey, the road had been my companion, and we developed a rather intimate relationship as minutes turned into hours and days transformed into weeks. We shared a dialogue that was more often a monologue because the road kept telling me its never-ending stories when mostly what I wanted was silence. The road would ask me questions about my past, my future, and my present. It would dig up my many errors and mistakes and invite me to reflect on all my former poor decisions and failures. However, sometimes—like a sage from another dimension—the road would reward me with epiphanies around my patterns and subconscious life. That's the thing about being on a pilgrimage—for all its trials, it gives you plenty of time to contemplate and learn to know yourself on a deeper level. As the veil of our identity gets increasingly thinner, we can move past our customary stories and actually hear what our heart wants to tell us.

In one of these moments on day twelve, the road (which until then had mostly been hanging around in a pleasant yet nonexpressive mode) suddenly decided to have its say: "You see that next bend over there?" it asked me. "Your curiosity and courage have carried you all this way to explore curve after curve after curve. The thing is, there's always more road for you to run. After the next curve, you'll find another one. You do know that you can keep going and searching forever, right?" After a pause, my inner voice (impersonating the road) spoke up again: "The pain ends when you make it end."

In that moment, scenes from my life (especially those involving my relationships) scrolled quickly by. I realized that the message I'd just heard from my subconscious held the keys to what I'd been searching for: Why had doing hard and extreme things come so naturally to me all my life? Why was I so good at being tough and not giving up? Suddenly, I realized the pattern between the moment at hand and the experience that ultimately had led me to this ultrarun in the first place: *It had always been easier for me to be hard on myself than to be gentle and merciful.*

Gentle power means to feel honestly into where we are regarding our strength.

I slowed down my pace (which was already quite slow at that point) to a near halt. *The pain ends when I make it end,* I repeated to myself. Even when faced with abuse, I had always chosen to take the hard way out and stay a little bit longer, over and over again, because it was in my nature to endure—and also because I was harboring hope of a positive outcome. The message I'd heard from myself was about choice. I couldn't change my past, but I could craft a new way of being in the future.

I took a day off. I went to the local ER with Mina to see a doctor—a man who happened to be an ultrarunner himself who had volunteered at Everest base camps to help climbers in distress. The doctor understood what I was trying to do, and we had a beautiful discussion about realistic options. So, after an honest look at what was going on with my pain (not a fracture as we feared, but swelling due to stress that we could manage with rest), I pivoted from only running to incorporating sections on a bicycle to allow my leg to heal and also bring more balance, joy, and harmony to the journey. I wasn't about to quit the trip, especially because we had several more events organized along the way. But I had arrived at a new place—it was more important for me to be happy and balanced than to be tough and finish seeing the run through as originally planned. I wanted to actually enjoy what I was doing. I wanted to honor the two years I'd put into preparing for the journey, and I wanted to honor my body and the people who were part of it.

Gentle power means to feel honestly into where we are regarding our strength. It doesn't mean to keep going no matter what so we can say we were right and succeed at all costs. In the past, my determination and sisu led me to stay in a relationship that was not only harmful to me, but outright dangerous. I was determined to help my partner heal from his demons and find peace, but I did so at the cost of my own mental and physical well-being. I knew I wasn't that person anymore. In this new chapter of my life, I could choose to push myself through the pain no matter what, or I could choose discernment and harmony. Nowadays, I'm happy to announce that I'm a student of the latter path. While our every-day life examples may not involve an ultrarun or an outrightly abusive relationship, there are times when we may harbor diminishing thoughts or patterns in our relationships that push us to keep on going regardless of cost. Noticing these moments, no matter how minute, are opportunities to calibrate to more gentleness and self-care.

On Walking Uphill

Annastiina Hintsa, an ultrarunner whose company coaches many of the world's top athletes as well as Fortune 500 CEOs, stopped on the road behind me. She called my name and continued: "Slow down! Otherwise, you'll just have to stand there and wait for me!" It was day one of our four-day ultramarathon. I had phoned Annastiina a month earlier to ask if she would run some 160 miles with me from Helsinki to Turku along the southwest coast of Finland for my first ever multiday test run.

I'd seen photos of Annastiina running in the Gobi Desert and Antarctica, and that qualified her as someone crazy and experienced enough for the task. I found out later that she wasn't just an incredible athlete, but she was also determined, kind, and full of good advice. "This might sound boring," she told me after we ran forty-five miles together in one day, "but I rec-ommend you walk when you go uphill. When you're doing an ultrarun of such ludicrous distance, as you will in New Zealand, you must run and simultaneously think about your recovery, not only for the next day but for the weeks and months to come. There's no sense in wasting energy by fighting gravity." Her advice proved invaluable for me later on in New Zealand. It might've even saved the whole trip because it allowed me to manage my energy more wisely. And just like most things we learn when we truly challenge ourselves, the lesson of slowing down when meeting a hill began to carry over into the rest of my life.

If you find yourself relentlessly keeping the same pace with work, family, friends, hobbies, and so on when life imposes a prolonged strain on you, consider that it might be time to slow down and walk for a while. Get some extra rest. Ask for help. It's okay to slow down, and sometimes we need to switch to just doing the bare minimum in order to rest and recover. When I first started trying out this approach myself, I literally started twitching if I wasn't running or on the move in some way. I actually had trouble understanding why some people enjoyed things like massages so much. That's luckily not the me of today, and I'm a much happier woman for it.

If we're constantly fighting gravity by pushing onward at the same pace when the road tilts up, we risk burning out our reserves and, ultimately, ourselves. We might manage to push through most of the time because the human body and mind are incredibly robust and resourceful. Even so, we can unintentionally undermine our ability to enjoy the journey and finish strong. Ultimately, when we exploit our inner reserves too much, there's always a check to pay. "Nothing is worth the stress, my love," I remember a close friend saying. He pointed at his chest that still a decade later bore the scars from a triple open-heart surgery.

We can do almost anything, but we can't do everything. Not learning how to infuse our power and strength with gentleness can very well lead to not finishing at all. I realized through my running that in a world that rewards us for looking good, always being strong, and constantly achieving, true power comes from forging your own reality and honoring your own pace. None of us need to stay seduced by messages to be a *good girl* or to *be the man*, especially when doing so often comes at the expense of our energy, health, relationships, and well-being. Choose your own pace. You might just discover that *less truly is more*.

CHAPTER 4:

The Paradox of Gentleness

There is nothing so strong as gentleness and
nothing so gentle as real strength.[1]

I t was day eleven in New Zealand, and I had been making my way up north along the South Island. Tired but resolute, I was approaching the town where we would camp that evening. Toward the end of the day, I had been in deep thought about my journey and stopped by a little gas station to rest my feet. I heard a vehicle slow down and finally come to a halt. The driver had recognized me from an article that *The New Zealand Herald* had run some weeks prior.[2] "Oh my gosh, it *is* you! I was telling my wife that it sure looks like the Finnish runner we read about. It's very inspiring what you are doing."

An entire family, along with a small dog, emerged from the van and surrounded me. I was tired and felt the mileage in my feet. However, the sweet man's excitement snapped me out of my tiredness. I welcomed him with my undivided presence, and he shared his experience of witnessing physical violence in his home as a young boy and later, emotional abuse in his previous relationship. After we finished talking, a teenage girl approached me and asked gently: "And how are you doing?" The thoughtfulness and surprise of her question moved me. I paused for a moment to feel her kind intent, and answered: "Thank you for asking," I said. "I am glad to be here, but I feel sad for the reason of my run." A simple exchange, but thanks to the astute question of the girl and my comfort to reveal my experience, along with the honest sharing by the father earlier, we experienced a sweet reminder of the beauty of welcoming each other just as we are and remaining human first.

Mistaking Gentleness as Weakness

Remember the friend I mentioned at the opening of chapter 2 who felt uncomfortable with my writing about power? Some people feel the same thing about gentleness. "Why do you have to write about that fluffy stuff?" a different friend asked me. "The world needs more courage, especially women. You should write more about us being in our power."

Most of us have been told a terrible lie our whole lives that anything soft, gentle, and supple (and feminine) is somehow inherently weak, unreliable, or of lesser value. This lie has caused untold suffering and has led to innumerable harmful decisions in politics and private organizations. For far too long, our culture has been overly infatuated with winning, competing, and making a profit, while gentleness and cooperation has been labeled *inferior* or *fragile*.

French philosopher André Comte-Sponville says that gentleness is "courage without violence, strength without harshness, love without anger" and also that "gentleness is gentleness only as long it owes nothing to fear."[3] Our inability to assert boundaries, our struggles to lead people, and our reluctance to express opinions because we fear rejection is not gentleness but meekness. Gentleness is not about being passive or always accommodating others. Gentleness is a way of moving forward with a kind of dynamic grace. It's about knowing when to push and when to pull back. It's about succeeding not through force, but through empowerment.

Far too many of us have been dealing with an out-of-whack nervous system for years. We've been hardwired to overreact, overextend, and overwork. Adopting the gentle power style of encountering the world and moving through it isn't so much about learning something new, but about unlearning these unhealthy ways of living. Gentle power is about finding accomplishment through nurturing a spirit of ease toward ourselves and others instead of achievement (no matter how glorious in the moment) and striving at the long-term cost of inner peace.

Comte-Sponville further describes gentleness as "a kind of peace, either real or desired . . . it can be pierced by anguish and suffering or brightened by joy and gratitude, but it is always devoid of hatred, harshness, and insensitivity."[4] Imagine if our experiences in leadership, social activism, politics, and families were devoid of harshness, force, and insensitivity. Imagine a relationship with yourself that's completely free from judgment and blame. Socially, we're told that this sort of treatment toward ourselves and others is soft and weak when it's actually empowering, constructive, and energizing.

Brené Brown is a bestselling author and well-known research professor at the University of Houston whose work focuses on understanding the concepts and lived experience of courage, shame, and vulnerability. She is often asked whether leaders who are authentic and brave should, in the name of vulnerability, bare all their emotions and processes. The answer in short is no. As Brown puts it, "Vulnerability without boundaries is not vulnerability."[5] The point, according to her, is not oversharing or full self-disclosure, but remaining present and leaning into feelings of fear and hard conversations when you feel uncertain, vulnerable, challenged, or at-risk. In this way, a leader is someone who truly feels the tension and keeps leading. As I mentioned in chapter 1, Rick Smith says this is about embracing the uncomfortable "charge inherent to being in charge" by having the courage to welcome anything that wants our attention. Vulnerability has been a hot commodity for a few years now. Like gentleness, vulnerability often belongs to the category of terms people overuse without infusing them with true substance. That's a shame because at their core, vulnerability and gentleness are acts of extreme strength; in moments of tension, despair, and stress, vulnerability and gentleness are what empower us to remain present, not succumb to the temptation to check out or slouch into our habitual shadow responses (such as avoidance, disconnection, and projection) when things get tough or we're tired. They allow us to lean into the moment and feel the fear in a grounded way, which means that we're less likely to discharge our tension and anxiety onto others. Vulnerability and gentleness also ensure that we don't abandon our own experience, which again ties into Rick Smith's notion of inner authority I mentioned at the end of chapter 1. It can be challenging to lead ourselves and our emotions sometimes, but with openness and curiosity, we can slowly learn to do so.

To Aristotle, gentleness was a virtue of temperance and the observance of mean between anger and "lack of spirit"—to not be led by emotion and "irascibility."[6] Comte-Sponville also comments that "gentleness in anger stands as the middle ground."[7] In the same way that vulnerability isn't about oversharing, gentleness isn't about overcaring or overextending ourselves. A gentleness that isn't informed by discernment and boundaries easily turns into fakeness, meekness, and boundless people-pleasing. In the words of Marcus Aurelius, "Gentleness is invincible, if it be genuine and not sneering or hypocritical. For what can the most insolent do to you, if you continue gentle to him and, if opportunity allows, mildly admonish him and quietly show him a better way at the very moment when he attempts to do you injury."[8]

Anne Dufourmantelle was a philosopher and psychoanalyst whose work covered a wide variety of subjects, including gentleness and risk-taking. She wrote that survival and danger are interrelated and warned against the pursuit of "absolute security."[9] Dufourmantelle's candid and courageous inquiry into gentleness further demonstrates what a complex theme we're dealing with. She asserts that the real obstacle to gentleness isn't necessarily what comes to mind first (harshness, violence, war, crime, and so on), but gentleness itself. Dufourmantelle is referring to the phony, fake, and passive gentleness that Comte-Sponville says "owes everything to fear" and therefore in fact becomes powerless. Gentleness is only real when it dares to face difficult situations and mental states like confusion, negativity, and fear. Only then does gentleness embrace the fullness of human experience.

Gentleness is an expression of audacity.

This paradox of gentleness relates to something I feel is expressed by Rainer Maria Rilke in *Letters to a Young Poet*: "Perhaps all the dragons of our lives are princesses who are only waiting to see us once beautiful and brave. Perhaps everything terrible is in its deepest being something helpless that wants helps from us."[10] That princess is the potential for fearlessness in all of us disguised as something terrible, just waiting for us to show up fully so that it can remove the masks of inauthenticity. Dufourmantelle herself died while living her purpose of gentle fearlessness—she was trying to save two children from drowning in turbulent waters near Saint-Tropez.

In a world that so often glorifies playing hard and tolerates self-serving authority, gentleness is always a risk. We're expected to be disciplined and strict, overextended to the point of burnout, and ever demanding of ourselves and others. Yet, gentleness and vulnerability are the keys to true power because they free us from the dreadful burden of pretense. To be as we appear and to appear as we are are the marks of inner authority and thus, conscious leadership. Following our intuition, slowing down, waiting patiently for what emerges, choosing mercy over control . . . all of these are approaches to leading one's life with gentle power.

Gentleness is an expression of audacity—at best, a fully expanded and unapologetic way of meeting the present moment. Gentleness means arriving at the edge of our sisu, taking a deep breath, opening our eyes wide to whatever is at hand, and doing so with curiosity and courage that are soft around the edges. Gentleness is approaching ourselves and others unmoved, grounded in uncompromising tenderness that still doesn't err on the side of excess in anything—not even in our amiability. Gentleness in challenging interactions with others is about recognizing the inherent ego-vulnerabilities in all of us and doing the best we can with the least amount of distress. Gentleness means that we thoroughly love one another, but we won't entertain dysfunctional behavioral patterns or rogue mental triggers.

Toward Uniarchy

Despite the research that supports the intuitive notion that relational transparency promotes greater well-being, productivity, creativity, increased life-expectancy, and reduced stress, mainstream approaches to leadership still undervalue qualities such as gentleness, empathy, and compassion. The legal industry in the West, in particular, is widely known for its toxic work culture. Nearly a third of all lawyers recently surveyed suffer from depression; almost a quarter report suffering from anxiety and/or alcoholism.[11] The constant demand to perform at such a high level without the requisite self-care doesn't merely come from within; its expected from leadership in law, health care, the corporate world, higher education, and so on. As you'll see later in the book, a different approach that values "soft" qualities like presence, warmth, empathy, and listening has been proven to foster innovation, creativity, productivity, and high performance in work environments and elsewhere.

Pixar is one of the most successful players in the creative field and movie business. Amy Edmondson describes how Ed Catmull, the retired head of Pixar, fostered an atmosphere of psychological safety in which employees were encouraged to share new ideas without fear of ridicule. She also shares that Catmull, by admitting his own fallibility, encouraged these attributes across the organization.[12] Is it any wonder that Pixar has garnered such fame, praise, and revenue over the past couple of decades? Twenty Academy Awards, nine Golden Globes, and a number of box office hits in a field where only half of the movies bring in a profit is more than noteworthy. In the case of Pixar, the company culture informed by gentleness delivered the milestones and returns that the capitalist business world ultimately seeks. Sadly, in the past, Pixar too had its crises of psychological trust, and in 2018, Catmull's cofounder and Pixar's chief creative director John Lasseter was let go of the company due to behavioral misconduct. As Edmondson writes in her book, "Lasseter's behavior and consequent outing underscores the fragile and temporal nature of psychological safety."[13]

Jane Dutton and her research team provide the study and example of Sarah Boidt who led a thirty-person billing department in a community hospital in Jackson, Michigan.[14] The department was positively deviant in a number of ways. Not only were they the best in the state in terms of the time it took to collect money, but they had low turnover as well as a waiting list of people who wanted to join the team. However, what was most remarkable was how people working for Boidt reported how they were growing, developing, and becoming better versions of themselves by working there. She had created an extraordinarily compassionate unit that at the same time was known for its high performance. Dutton describes Boidt as a great listener, humble, empowering, and wise about the importance of creating care between people within the unit and with partners outside the unit. She was very playful too. The unit regularly had squirt-gun fights and other elaborate forms of spontaneous play.[15]

This all being said, why is it that people bemoan toxic and self-serving leaders while still following and even protecting them? Why do softness, warmth, and compassion continue to be dismissed, rejected, and ridiculed? Why does gentleness as an aspect of leadership push our buttons so much?

A couple of years ago, I traveled to northern China to study kung fu, tai chi, and Eastern philosophy, specifically to learn millennia-old practices to cultivate mental focus and tranquility. In Taoism, the rhythm of life pulsates endlessly through the entire universe. It's the action of the two complementary (not opposing, as it is sometimes misunderstood) principles of yin and yang. Yin energy is thought of as soft and feminine energy, whereas yang is hard and masculine. It's important to note that these two energies are not gendered per se, and everyone is comprised of a flowing combination of both. According to Chinese medicine, it's the imbalance of these energies that creates the ailments we experience in our physical and mental worlds. The inherent nature of yang energy (or *form*) envisions, plans, directs, and builds. Its qualities are hierarchy, order, logic, and linearity. Yang is more about doing than being. Yin (or *formlessness*) is about being and creative intuition. Its inherent nature is feeling, non-linearity, spirality, and nurturance.

I asked a teacher in China why the world seems to prefer masculine energy and why we tend to glorify hard qualities while deeming softness as weak. He said that it was perhaps that yang energy appeals to the masses, especially during uncertain times. Yang reassures us with its direction and clarity, and that's great. Unless that direction is the wrong one, of course. My teacher offered a telling metaphor: yang designs and builds the structure for a beautiful house or dojo; yin brings the lights, flowers, atmosphere, and life into the building and makes it worth inhabiting. Just as a structure needs both types of energies, my teacher said, so does the world. He called the artful blending of yin and yang *uniarchy*.

I'd never heard the word before, but I liked it. To truly succeed in life, we need to embrace the uniarchy of both qualities, and that's the only approach that will bring harmony to the world. In other words, the future isn't feminine or masculine. The future calls for the union of these two energies and leadership styles in every person, and both need to be respected for their unique qualities. Imbalanced yin leadership lacks direction and safety; it's overwhelming and chaotic. On the other hand, imbalanced yang leadership turns rigid and dogmatic; it lacks sensitivity and the ability to navigate with care.

The first time I heard the expression *feminine leadership* was from Stephane Leblanc in the fall of 2016. I was visiting Montreal for a conference I was speaking at, and I met Stephane at a little restaurant nearby. His face had a beaming and welcoming energy as he greeted me with a massive hug. Stephane's demeanor always communicated determination and grace in a way that felt inspiring. He was an entrepreneur and leadership trainer with a couple of decades behind him in the corporate world as a vice president and general manager of two different transportation industry companies. Stephane had felt like an outsider in that work because he'd been determined to bring what he called *conscious leadership* into those organizations. So he left to found the International Centre for Conscious Leadership to be a catalyst for the transformation of leaders and the elevation of consciousness in business.

I knew Stephane for about six years. To the immense shock to me and countless others whose life he touched, Stephane died unexpectedly and well before I had a chance to interview him for this book. When the news of his untimely death reached me, I grieved for him like I would for a family member. That morning when I heard the news, I'd spoken with a friend about examples of gentle power amidst all the chaos of leadership we're witnessing these days, and Stephane was one of the first people I thought of. Through his generosity, gentleness, and grit—while being very human and heartfelt at the same time—Stephane was gentle power embodied, and his grace is missed by those who knew him. In a message he wrote me in September 2017, Stephane said, "Love is the most powerful force there exists in the universe." It was Stephane's love for both the gentle and strong within us, as well as his dream to support a kind of leadership, the uniarchy, that unites these two, that left a legacy that will carry beyond his time on earth. I've dedicated this book to Stephane to acknowledge his dream and so his two lovely children will know that their father's vision helped point the way forward for all of us.

Sometimes it's easier to recognize the power and impact of something by its absence. Stephane's message primed me to be on the lookout for what was missing in my life—the courage to not always be so tough. As paradoxical as life can be, as I shared in chapter 3, I ended up discovering gentleness for myself in perhaps one of the most unexpected places I could ever imagine: during a ludicrous cross-country run that was supposed to be all about toughness. Turns out things aren't always what they seem.

CHAPTER 5:

The Science of the Good Heart

Although the world is full of suffering,
it is also full of the overcoming of it.

–HELEN KELLER

previously mentioned Sarah Boidt, whose success at creating flourish-ment among her team in the sticky world of debt collection is a telling example of what can come from introducing gentleness into leadership. Another story was relayed to me by Emma Seppälä, who's the author of *The Happiness Track* and faculty director at Yale School of Management. I contacted Emma for another real-life example of a leader who has used gentleness and kindness in their everyday leadership and is reaping the benefits—which are measurable in hard numbers. She didn't hesitate a moment as she told me about Ashley Bernardi, the founder and CEO of media relations firm Nardi Media. Emma shared that Ashley saw her business revenue double in the span of two years, from six to seven figures—despite the economic challenges caused by the pandemic—mainly as a result of a change in how she was leading herself and thus, her company.

After experiencing a debilitating form of Lyme disease in 2016 cou-pled with serious postpartum depression after the birth of her third child, Ashley's recovery paved the way for a deeper sense of understanding for others. As she integrated her post-traumatic growth discoveries of com-passion and empathy into her leadership, her business returns beautifully reflected this change. Ashley established new company core values, which include family and kindness, and as an act of self-care and to set an example, for the first time in her life, Ashley made caring for her own physical and emotional well-being a nonnegotiable part of her daily life.

She took up a regular practice of meditation, breathwork, and yoga, and very importantly, she prioritized good sleep. Ashley describes her transformation in her book, *Authentic Power: Give Yourself Permission to Feel,* and shares in an interview: "When I learned to put myself first, I saw transformation happen in my life in the most powerful ways: I attracted like-minded team members who lifted each other up and aligned with my core values, one of them being kindness. Our business flourished."[1]

In the words of Daniel Goleman—psychologist, science journalist, and award-winning pioneer in the field of emotional intelligence, "Leaders skilled at empathy are not 'soft.' They're smart at using a powerful leadership tool."[2] Indeed, according to the most cutting-edge organizational research, the future of leadership will be based on the so-called *soft skills* of empathy, compassion, and emotional intelligence, in addition to STEM (science, technology, engineering, and mathematics). According to Goleman, soft skills also include self-awareness, self-regulation, motivation, empathy, and social skills, whereas *tough skills* pertain to traits such as intelligence, analytical and technical skills, determination, rigor, and vision. Soft skills are invaluable because they help leaders communicate clearly and receive input from others with sensitivity. By now, the evidence is more than clear: emphasizing human connection works. Leading with that in mind not only makes us feel happier; it offers the best results.

So why haven't we made the shift sooner? In a study from 2013, Joan Marques—a professor at Woodbury University's School of Business—concluded that overemphasizing tough or hard skills and restraining the value of the above-mentioned soft skills has led to widely accepted ideas that leadership should be about boldness, charisma, and superior knowledge.[3] Marques points out that this approach has been adopted not only in corporate environments, but in business schools as well, perpetuating the flow of tough, skill-focused entrants into the workforce. The challenge, according to Marques, is to convince these leaders to reestablish their internal balance—a balance that has been systematically skewed to one side in their formal education.

The notion of balance isn't new by any measure. In particular, Taoists have been encouraging us to focus on the harmony between hard and soft for over two thousand years. "This is called subtle and obscure insight,"

Lao Tzu writes. "Therefore, the place of what is firm and strong is below, and that of what is soft and weak is above."[4] *Tao Te Ching* elevates the principle of *softness*, not pushing or asserting, as the ultimate undercurrent of all action, encouraging that one must continue to know yang, but remember to abide in yin. Power alone doesn't cut it; we must learn to use it with compassion, grace, and love. Harmony is everything. "If princes and kings were able to maintain it, all things would of themselves be transformed by them," Lao Tzu continues.

Psychological research certainly supports this idea.[5] When our parasympathetic nervous system (the *rest and digest* system) is active, we're relaxed; when we're relaxed—or, in other words, in a neurological state of trust and safety—we're more creative, innovative, and have better access to our cognitive-action repertoire. In turn, that empowers superior problem-solving skills, better memory and health, more satisfying relationships, and even greater longevity. Gentleness isn't just a nice thing to do; it's clearly the best approach to take. Researchers like Marques and Goleman are proponents of the gentle approach because studies indicate that it yields better results than the traditional "tough boss" method of leadership.[6] In simple terms, people admire and trust leaders who show them kindness, and that in turn boosts overall performance. Children learn better as well when they experience safety and freedom from judgment. This works because positive emotions and psychological states, such as joy, contentment, trust, pride, and love, broaden our decision and action repertoires, which builds our enduring personal resources—physically, intellectually, socially, and psychologically.

A Million Dollar Discovery

In 2012, Google started Project Aristotle—a study of 180 of their teams to understand why some stumbled while others performed brilliantly.[7] The researchers began by reviewing a half a century of academic studies on how teams work. Were the best teams made up of people with similar interests, or were diversity and communication skills the key? How about incentives for good work, gender balance, and educational background? These were all good guesses, but the researchers had a hard time finding any definitive pattern. In fact, the *who* aspect of the team success equation didn't seem to matter so much.

Three years into their study, the team stumbled upon Amy Edmondson's research on psychological safety. Edmondson, whom I mentioned in chapter 4, is the Novartis professor of leadership and management at Harvard Business School, and she's been called the *mother of psychological safety* for her pioneering work on the topic. Edmondson's early studies focused on the effects of teamwork on medical error rates. What she found puzzled her. Opposite to what she expected, the higher-performing teams also reported higher error rates.[8] Ultimately, this led Edmondson to surmise that maybe those teams didn't actually make more mistakes; maybe they were just more able and willing to talk about them. This inquiry is what led her to discover the power of psychological safety.

The Google team, inspired by Edmondson's work, ran their analysis again, and the results were clear: the highest-performing teams shared the belief that the team was safe for interpersonal risk-taking. They didn't fear embarrassment, rejection, or punishment for speaking up. The construct of psychological safety dates back to the organizational research of Edgar Schein and Warren Bennis in 1965.[9] But it was Edmondson's research that identified such an interpersonal climate as being conducive to interpersonal risk-taking and therefore to creativity and innovation on the team.[10] Catmull, who I presented earlier, defined this as *candor*. According to Edmondson, this is what was enacted at Pixar by meetings with smart and passionate people to solve problems in an environment that encourages everyone to be fully honest and open with each other.

Positive emotions, like trust, safety, and acceptance, allow us to loosen our grip on fundamental survival.

Matt Lieberman is a social scientist who has researched the neuroscience of human connection. According to Lieberman, phrases such as "you broke my heart" are way more than overused metaphors—for the brain, the pain we experience from rejection is just as real as physical pain.[11] His research, too, indicates that social connection for humans is a necessity, not a luxury. For this reason, humans evolved to pick up on (or at least evolved with a built-in proclivity for understanding) other people's emotions. This, according to Lieberman, is our superpower when it comes to connection, cocreation, and collaboration.

Research also shows that threat wreaks havoc on how our brains process external cues and information.[12] In a phenomenon called the *amygdala hijack*, fear disconnects us from the prefrontal cortex and allows the evolutionarily older part of our brains—the limbic system—to take over. When this occurs, we struggle to make complex decisions and maintain more than one perspective. Looking back on stressful events, we might even have difficulty remembering the details of what we said. We know, too, that positive emotions, like trust, safety, and acceptance, allow us to loosen our grip on fundamental survival, which enables us to access our cognitive capacities in full.

Even though we're all ultimately responsible for our emotions, our evolutionary hardwiring has bestowed us with the ongoing need to feel safe. According to the stated research, when we feel safe with our peers and feel like we can trust them, we tend to be more creative, productive, healthy, happy, and fulfilled. This doesn't mean that it's my duty to ensure that no one ever feels discomfort, which would be an impossible task anyway. We all have our triggers and sensitive spots that may sometimes show up regardless of how others behave around us. As I describe later in the chapter, this is centrally influenced by our attachment style, which has its roots all the way in our first experiences of connecting with our caretakers. However, when I choose to interact with gentleness, I do my part in fostering a more welcoming space for connection.

On the other hand, when we express harshness, are merciless, or are judgmental about others, it wreaks havoc in the areas of human engagement better served by more trust, openness, and safety. Edmondson shares that psychological safety isn't some new concept or magic bullet, but that it is undeniably "the underpinning of everything at a workplace." Open communication, she notes, is difficult to measure, but the absence of such can result in terrible organizational failures.[13] For example, studies of black box voice recordings from crashed passenger airliners regularly reveal that the fear or reluctance to contradict a senior leader (the first pilot, in this case) can spell the difference between life and death.[14]

While the consequences of holding back information crucial to making fully informed decisions in the corporate or family arena aren't likely as dramatic, these studies illustrate the fact there is a definite cost when people don't feel free to share. The environment we create cues our emotional radar in a fraction of a second. Although the human brain has tripled in size over the past seven million years or so, its function remains the same: to make sure we stay alive. No matter how clever, courageous, or charismatic we might be, there isn't a power more influential in our lives than our inherent need to feel safe, and it's matched only by the power of making others feel safe in our presence.

The Future Begins with an Idea

The workforce is increasingly living in what's known as a *knowledge economy*, meaning that the knowledge employees bring with them into the organization (in the form of education and unique life experiences, for example) is what truly adds value to that organization. With this in mind, it's staggering that in many companies, half of the employees report that they can't speak up at work.[15] With each idea that goes unshared, potential value is lost. Apart from the organizational world, just think of all the books that were never written, all the startups that were never founded, all the talent that was never developed and displayed because of someone feeling that they couldn't share what was on their mind. All of us can recall at least one moment in life in which we didn't follow our desire because we feared how others would react. Research shows that the one thing people fear nearly as much as death is public speaking—not because microphones are inherently terrifying or crowds of people are necessarily traumatic, but because most of us are keenly sensitive to feeling disregarded, humiliated, or rejected.[16]

Lauri Järvilehto, a professor of practice at Aalto University in Finland, has written several books on a variety of topics (learning, philosophy, intuition, and entrepreneurship among them). "The future is always first an idea," he once told me over lunch. I had just rejected his idea of me doing a doctorate on sisu, mainly because I didn't like the sound of being stuck at any university for five-plus years. Then Lauri suggested I do the program in Finland where the system allows for more independence than, for example, in the US. This was one thought that—initially rejected—was allowed to take root and alter more than one life along the way. But it was only because I had a support system of caring friends to help me feel safe enough to give it a shot.

I didn't know it at the time, but Lauri would become one of the advisors for my doctorate, and the two of us would also collaborate in creating an entire "Year of Sisu" in Finland (which included us cocreating a book on sisu together, organizing two major public events, and plastering all the main bus stops between Lapland and Helsinki with posters encouraging our fellow Finns to dig into their sisu in the midst of dark winter). In other words, we never know how far an idea might take us. This book, too, is in some ways the result of the conversation Lauri and I had while having a casual lunch.

The problem is that everyone has great ideas, but the opportunity to realize them isn't universal. As everyday leaders, that's up to us. We need to not only seek how to support brilliant ideas, but how to foster the types of environments in which they can sprout and be shared.

The Power of Positive Emotions

While the work of Dacher Keltner suggests that the more powerful an individual becomes, the more their empathy tends to decrease, research on emotional intelligence also shows that empathy is a crucial trait that makes leaders and their organizations more effective, encourages positive team climates, and increases employee retention. Research into the social neuroscience of empathy further proposes that empathy works because it's an essential aspect of informed decision-making in complex situations, and it acts as a buffer against the cold, impersonal, and dehumanized business practices that affect everyone.[17]

Chapter 4's epigraph ("There is nothing so strong as gentleness and nothing so gentle as real strength") conveys a sobering message to our profit-obsessed world about the gentle power of what we consider to be soft and supple. It is not an energy that pushes, cajoles, or forces, but one that invites, inspires, and empowers, and that's why its long-term impact is so unmatched.

Matt Trainer elaborates in a beautifully down-to-earth way why gentle leadership is so powerful and yet so ordinary:

> Strong communities form when leaders show care and invest in the success of their reports. Showing care means that the leader can gently navigate all of the various emotions that life triggers for an individual, because they all happen at work. There's euphoria and heartbreak, excitement and jealousy, friendship and rivalry. Leaders who enroll in supporting individuals through all these ups and downs inspire their people to higher performance, selflessness, and loyalty. These are the foundations of communities where people thrive and consistently outperform other teams.[18]

Similarly, Anne Dufourmantelle writes that "gentleness invents an expanded present."[19] Gentleness acts as an expansive ingredient because it primes us for safety, which in turn nourishes our cognitive reserves. Barbara Fredrickson—a psychology professor and director of the Positive Emotions and Psychophysiology Laboratory at UNC–Chapel Hill—described this phenomenon in 1998.[20] Her seminal study demonstrates how negative emotions are different from positive emotions in that they trigger the nervous system's threat response. This response narrows our perception (quite literally narrowing our visual field, as Fredrickson and her team discovered) and limits access to our ability to process information and to cognitive reserves. Emotions that trigger our fight-or-flight-response mechanism disrupt executive function and put us in scarcity mode by transferring our decision-making over to the limbic system, which is hardwired for survival at all costs. Fredrickson's work on the power of positive emotions is a sister to Edmondson's findings on psychological safety. Not having to worry about being punished, ridiculed, or attacked for one's ideas or mistakes mitigates the trigger-happy flight-or-fight mode and activates our parasympathetic rest response, which drives the expansive function of positive emotions.

A conscious discussion about sisu, resilience, achievement, and productivity (or any of the like in today's volatile and complex world) cannot happen without acknowledging the crucial role of leadership in managing psychological safety as well as understanding the hard facts around the importance of positive emotions and human behavior, creativity, well-being, and the ability to thrive in the face of hardships. By now, we're familiar with the high cost of our constantly quickening pace of life, cut-throat competition, a profit-over-well-being mindset, prioritizing force over healthy power, and simply ignoring how to create life-giving environments for each other.

According to 2019 statistics (notably before the pandemic), 55 percent of Americans are stressed during the day, which is about 20 percent higher than the global average. Of those who experience stress, 57 percent report being paralyzed by it.[21] Data from the American Institute of Stress shows that an overwhelming majority (80 percent) are stressed as a result of work, and nearly a third report in another study from 2018 that the main source of their stress is their boss.[22] In a survey by the American Psychological Association in 2011, only 43 percent of respondents felt their employers cared about their work-life balance and took it into consideration.[23]

Low-quality connections leave damage in their wake.

Jane Dutton puts it this way: "The extent of incivility in the work-place is indeed disturbing: 90 percent of respondents in one poll believed workplace incivility was a serious problem, and 75 percent of respondents in another survey said it was getting worse. According to another study, one-third of six hundred nurses had been verbally abused during their previous five days at work."[24] Dutton is a distinguished professor of business administration and psychology at the University of Michigan. Her passion translates beautifully into her work on compassion and the difference it makes for individuals and organizations. Dutton's groundbreaking dedication to understanding the determinants of well-being and flourishing offer us yet another central construct to explore in the form of what she calls high-quality connections (HQC).[25] Dutton's theory postulates that every dyad of people entails avenues of connection that work not unlike blood vessels that carry nutrition. These avenues are like dynamic, living tissue that transport information, energy, and the codes to sensing whether the connection is elevating and safe or unsafe and diminishing.

These are the avenues through which gentle power is communicated. When it comes to Dutton's high-quality connections, it's the *quality* aspect that defines it as either life-giving or life-depleting. Low-quality connections leave damage in their wake. Dutton writes that "corrosive connections are like black holes: they absorb all the light in the systems and give back nothing in return."[26] She has researched HQCs in organizational contexts and suggests that they unlock spirals of positivity, meaning that their benefits carry far beyond the moments in which they occur. Similarly, Fredrickson refers to *positivity resonance*, which is like HQCs of mutual care and synchrony that have been associated with better mental health, resilience, and greater access to social resources.[27]

Dutton encourages us to consciously foster HQCs in all our daily relationships, whether with someone delivering a package to our door, a family member, or a colleague on the other end of a Zoom call. These connections are opportunities to produce resources in that they give us more life both in the moment and beyond: we feel more vitality, aliveness, and positive regard, which then encourages a cascade of elevating outputs. Connecting in these ways can involve looking at someone in a way that highlights their value and worth, actively listening to what they are saying, and consciously and respectfully choosing to engage with them from a place of good will.

Positive engagement is indeed one of the factors of systems intelligence (described in chapter 14) proposed by two Finnish Aalto University Professors, Raimo Hämäläinen and Esa Saarinen. We express positive engagement through the tone of our voice, the way we listen (or don't), the overall manner in which we move through the dynamic swirl of social systems, and the quality of our communication and engagement. This is what gentle power asks of us. By doing so, we create safe, empowering, and welcoming environments that naturally bring out the best in all of us.

Attachment Styles and Everyday Life

I want to end this chapter with a topic that underpins all our interactions, especially when we feel challenged. It also influences our access to gentle power.

Some years ago, I was walking along the boardwalk in Venice Beach and noticed a brown-haired young woman on rollerblades. She wore colorful braids and a black T-shirt that said in bold white letters: *Blame It on the Parents*. Whatever "it" was, I remember thinking that at least Sigmund Freud would have been pleased with her choice of costume. Although we can't blame every little bit of our struggle on our parents, psychological research resoundingly asserts that our early experiences with primary caretakers have a profound impact on our relationship skills as adults. Whether at home or the office, our basic human needs for acceptance, safety, and survival drive our style of engagement with each other.

Relational researchers and theorists call our various approaches to meeting these needs *attachment styles*. Understanding the factors that contribute to them—as well as our related experiences of anxiety, avoidance, and fulfillment—is critical when it comes to understanding our interactions with others. Why do we repeat the same dynamics and conflicts with some people and not with others? Why do we feel revulsed by some relationships and inexplicably hooked by others? Understanding our relational blueprint isn't a recipe for getting rid of unpleasant encounters outright, but it does help us see ourselves and others with much more clarity and understanding.

Diane Poole Heller describes how our attachment style influences all of our intimate relationships, especially in the ways we offer and seek comfort and security.[28] Attachment styles directly pertain to our experience of gentle power because they determine how we relate both to power and love—how we might overuse power or give it away, how conscious and honest we are when doing so, how open we are to love, and how we go about caring for others. Understanding our attachment style brings clarity to things like our fear of abandonment, codependency, and the ways we may manipulate others to ensure that our psychological needs for attachment are met.

Attachment styles are essentially patterns of relating that most of us have had since early childhood, when our developing egos were first learning to navigate the world and protect us from its imperfections. These patterns seek to be witnessed and released so the psychic energy they hold can be transferred to other essential functions. Since our attachment styles formed so early in life, they often operate in adulthood on a primal level without our full awareness. For that reason, it serves us to have at least a basic understanding of them, simply because they inform how we relate to everything we encounter—power, love, conflicts, generosity, boundaries, and so on. If you've ever wondered why your partner reacts so strongly when you show up slightly late (and it's no big deal to you), or why you find it so difficult to say no to people even when you're already spread so thin, or why you have a history of attracting emotionally unavailable people into your inner circle, or why you habitually have trouble sympathizing with your partner's emotional reactions, your attachment style may offer clues to understanding it.

John Bowlby was a psychoanalyst who outlined the theories of relational attachment, partially based on the earlier work of Harry Harlow. Bowlby asserted that our attachment responses are instinctual and hardwired over generations to prepare us for potential threats and to ensure survival.[29] They constitute an *attachment behavioral system* that guides us in forming and maintaining relationships, be they intimate, parental, professional, or—with particular relevance to this book—more in the realm of leadership and followership. The work of Cindy Hazan and Philip Shaver in organizational research indicates that the same attachment dynamics prevalent in intimate and family relationships also play out in our relationships with coworkers, leaders, and followers.[30]

It's important to view attachment styles as overarching patterns of behavior, rather than as personality types. In brief, attachment styles can be broken down into two primary categories: secure and insecure. *Secure attachment* is the ability to form relationships based on trust and mutual intimacy as well as the tendency to give and receive love with relative ease (and without becoming overly dependent or insecure when those close to us need time away). Securely attached individuals, which is roughly about half of the population, are generally least likely to fear failure or rejection. *Insecure attachment* typically includes three substyles of attachment. Although different theorists use different labels for them, the three can be thought of existing on a continuum of insecure responsiveness to intimacy, with *anxious* (or *ambivalent*) on one end, *fearful avoidant* (or *disorganized*) in the middle, and *dismissive avoidant* (or simply *avoidant*) on the other end.

The anxiously attached style is defined by a fear of abandonment that can show up as neediness and the longing for ongoing validation.

According to other research by Hazan and Shaver, about one fifth of those studied display this attachment style.[31] Avoidant attachment, on the other hand (and decidedly on the far end of the continuum), is marked by resistance to intimacy. Avoidant people tend to have a hard time letting people close (unlike anxious avoidants, who tend to develop strong emotions quickly) and expressing their most intimate feelings. Hazan and Shaver's work found that about a quarter of the adults studied possessed this attachment style. The third category can be viewed as a combination of the two subsets described above (which is one reason that some theorists prefer the term *disorganized*). Individuals with a fearful avoidant attachment style may exhibit contradictory reactions—although they yearn for intimacy, they also display resistance to intimate bonds. I once saw another girl with a T-shirt that had *YES!* printed on the front and *NO!* on the back. Fearful avoidants can come off a bit like this. All in all, most people tend to display a mix of all the patterns described above, but usually have a go-to style they resort to when feeling under-resourced or triggered.

Understanding our attachment styles—as well as how our nervous systems have evolved primarily to protect us from danger—can help us make sense of our own behavior and that of others. It can also help us comprehend the underlying needs that drive us all, particularly when our behaviors seem irrational or out of place. Although attachment styles are well-known within psychology, they don't seem to be discussed widely enough in the broader culture. I commonly employ attachment styles in my coaching work, only to receive curious looks from my clients. Invariably, though, the attachment frame is an extremely helpful tool that people wish they'd come across sooner in life. Just as Google Maps and similar apps have utterly changed the way we navigate the world, so will understanding our attachment styles, especially when it comes to navigating the sometimes-confusing terrain of our relationships. While diving into the deep end of attachment theory is beyond the scope of this book, I offer it here as a bookmark in case you wish to follow up on it. If you do choose to explore attachment styles, I can promise that it will offer you another useful tool for your personal growth.

To a great number of attachment theorists, like Poole Heller, learning about our particular style isn't so much about fixing ourselves; it's more about gaining self-understanding. Every time we increase our self-knowledge, we bring something useful into consciousness, which ide-ally means a wider array of useful options. The path of gentle power is in part based on becoming more aware of our inner programming, and that allows us to favor empowerment over thoughts and behaviors that no longer serve us. Understanding our inner blueprint and its associated behavioral patterns is an unparalleled tool for encouraging happiness, ease, and fulfillment in our lives and the lives of others. Every time we get to know something about ourselves—be it our aversion or craving for power, our boundaries and sense of sovereignty, or our fears and desires—we become more of who we truly are, and that in itself is fundamental to both healthy attachment and gentle power.

PART III

Fortitude

CHAPTER 6:

The Serendipitous Road to Sisu

*Don't be too timid and squeamish about your
actions. All life is an experiment.*

–RALPH WALDO EMERSON[1]

My personal journey with sisu began from the moment I was born in the dead of winter in Finland. While the exact moment of my entry into this world was rather uneventful (unless you consider that my dear mother was in labor for twenty-three hours), right after birth I was placed in an incubator in an effort to help me fight off a hospital-acquired infection. My sisu got the upper hand that time, as it has several times over the course of my life. However, it wasn't until much later when I was in my thirties, that my life would fully align with that fateful four-letter word, even though—just like millions of other Finns—I'd grown up hearing about sisu on a regular basis. It happened at University of Pennsylvania. I'd just walked into an Introduction to Positive Psychology class at the Annenberg auditorium with a bunch of students who, like myself, were quickly hooked on the topic and its engaging, razor-sharp professor. That professor was Angela Duckworth.

I was unfamiliar with Angela when I joined the class. That first day, she spoke to us about grit—the subject of her famous research. Her work immediately reminded me of sisu, although I knew that "grit" wasn't simple a translation of the term I knew so well. I couldn't help but walk over to the speaker podium after class to thank her and nervously introduce myself. Angela looked at me with her inquisitive and intelligent eyes, greeted me warmly, and said, "You're the first Finnish person I've ever met." Later that same day, I sent her an email to ask if she had heard of sisu. Of course, she had. Angela then added, "Who knows? Maybe one day you'll write your master's thesis on the subject."

My studies into sisu have been twofold from the beginning: First, I've been motivated to understand how humans overcome extreme adversity. Second, since adversity is so prominent in the human experience, I've been curious to find ways in which we can turn adversity into fuel (sort of like the ongoing effort to transform plastic waste into renewable energy). Originally, I'd written my applied positive psychology master's thesis proposal on the revolutionary theory of systems intelligence. Little did I know that Angela would later prompt me further to reconsider my master's thesis topic, even going so far to offer to be my thesis advisor.

Inspired by my stellar mentor-to-be and equipped with the insight and determination I'd gained from life experiences, I dove into the relatively uncharted realm of sisu. After years of struggle and headwind, life was seemingly becoming an open road for me, but it wasn't long until the doubts started rolling in. Who was I to talk about sisu? It was such a prestigious and dear concept to Finland. Shouldn't someone more experienced and older be doing this work? I was worried my fellow Finns would scoff at my attempts to unlock the centuries-old secrets of sisu. Even worse, they'd outright laugh at me.

Fortunately, I had Angela to lean on. She's worked in the demanding American university system and currently runs her own psychology research lab at University of Pennsylvania. On top of it all, Angela is a mother of two. She's known untold doubt and pressure, and she's witnessed her students get over their impediments and hesitations, year after year. When I told her my concerns, she barely batted an eye. "You don't need to be right about everything," she told me. "You just need to do your thing and be honest." Those words have remained my North Star ever since.

Why Sisu? Why Gentle Sisu?

Despite our huge advancements in space exploration, medicine, technology, and social sciences, surprising gaps remain in our understanding of the human spirit behind so much of this progress. Over one hundred years ago,

William James drew attention to the idea of an energy within people that became activated when faced with crisis. He called it the *second wind* and proposed creating an entire topography to understand it, similar to those that ophthalmologists use when scanning eyes.[2]

Let's say you're in a hurry, rushing so you don't miss your flight or train. You're just about at your destination, when suddenly you're faced with one of those painstakingly slow revolving doors you sometimes see in office buildings and hotels. You've dashed elegantly past countless people on your way just to encounter this absurd contraption, heart pounding as you wait for a tiny crack of an opening so you can squeeze yourself inside the cramped, revolving door and wait again to get past this hindrance. I often think of adversity like that. Everything's going fine until suddenly it isn't. Obstacles like these are universal in that everyone has to face them and slow down to figure them out from time to time.

Challenges are the great equalizers. No matter who we are—nationality, gender, social standing, or political ideology—we all stand naked and wounded in the face of grief, loss, severe illness, and the million types of trauma that humans face day in and day out. But adversity isn't merely an undesirable impediment to life. Adversity is what helps us experience life more fully and discover that we have more strength and fire within us than we thought, and this is a capacity that all of us share. And when we pause to witness our fellow humans' triumphs over hardship, we come to know our humanity's shared capacity for dignity and strength even more. This is what my research into sisu is all about—understanding our vulnerability, but more so our power and resiliency.

Sisu is another tool for us to liberate our latent powers and raise our collective ability to take action for the good of the whole. Because sisu relates to elementary facets of existence we all share, it can help us focus more on unity than division. That being said, sisu isn't a miracle cure. Some traits (courage, for example) are commonly thought of as positive, but the truth is that they also have shadow sides (foolhardiness, in this case) that are responsible for truly unfavorable outcomes. As Comte-Sponville notes, "the most suspect thing about courage is its indiscrimination: it can serve good or evil ends without changing their nature."[3] In the same way, Descartes says that humility can be either virtuous or vicious.[4] In a similar manner, sisu can manifest as beneficial or harmful. How any capacity ends up being characterized depends on how we use it, and how we use sisu depends on our values, belief systems, and behavioral patterns. For that reason, sisu and gentle power are ultimately a matter of self-discovery.

> Sisu is about expressing who we truly are in
> a way that makes a positive difference.

The most well-known images of sisu from Finland are rather one-dimensional—Finnish soldiers in the Winter War defending the country against the invading Soviet Red Army, fighting for their lives in the freezing cold during one of the harshest winters in history. Women and men, relentless in their duties, stern, silent, showing no weakness, and asking for no help. If you're familiar with the concept of sisu, this makes sense. What would *gentle sisu* even look like? And does a concept like *soft toughness* even make sense?

Of course, it does. We can be oriented toward getting things done and toughening through hardship without glorifying harsh, hurtful strength. A thoughtful discussion about a warmer kind of sisu requires that we question narratives that exalt power and winning at all costs—namely, the costs to others, to nature, and to our own well-being. In fact, it's qualities like grace, balance, attunement, and empathy that make sisu so vital. Keeping this in mind allows us to navigate adversity, uncertainty, and even chaos with less fear and a bit more openness, intuition, and wisdom. Sisu isn't just about survival. Nor is it just about overcoming challenges and coming out the other side no matter what. Sisu is about expressing who we truly are in a way that makes a positive difference.

The Obstacle Is the Way

Janur Yasa is a respected Balinese community leader and aikido teacher whose dedication to "the way of the peaceful warrior" inspired him to build a traditional Japanese dojo inside the premises of his restaurant *Moksa*, hidden away amidst some of the most picturesque rice paddies of Ubud,

Bali. We were both invited as speakers to a panel on sustainability and resilience, and Janur was answering a question from the audience regarding how to find the courage to follow impossible dreams. He sat next to me on stage, brown eyes glimmering, with the timeless, resolved look of someone who has faced the storms of severe illness, who has built an award-winning restaurant from scratch, and who has practiced aikido for more than a decade. When someone like Janur replies by saying, "The obstacle is the way," the message lands in my heart and reinvigorates me to remember my own resourcefulness and courage.

Nearly two thousand years ago, Marcus Aurelius wrote, "For the mind converts and changes every hindrance to its activity into an aid; and so that which is a hindrance is made a furtherance to an act; and that which is an obstacle on the road helps us on this road."[5] Aurelius set down these words and his other famous "meditations" in order to improve upon himself. He was a legendary leader who didn't simply hold on to the power he was given through his lineage as an aristocrat, or because he turned back invaders, or because he dealt with millions of his people dying from smallpox. Aurelius earned his power also through relentless inquiry into the ways of leading, becoming a better person, discovering how to better manage adversity, as well as how to rein in emotions and focus on what matters most. Just like Aurelius, we all have a masterpiece like *Meditations* that's unique to us, and it's revealed to us partially through how we navigate challenge and hardship. For Finns, this masterpiece goes by the name *sisu*.

The takeaway for leaders is this: that which causes you, your organization, or your community the most fear can be your greatest gift. It's also how you can forge positive meaning out of the uncertainty and hardship you will invariably face. The takeaway for parents (and others of us leading ourselves through the small and large moments of everyday relationships) is that through these relationships, we can learn to forge a more empowering presence for the people whose well-being ultimately matters everything.

Leadership is one of the most courageous, demanding, and—in my opinion—rewarding paths to self-discovery. Just as parenthood or any other relationship intimate enough to regularly pose a threat to our ego, leadership has a way of undressing our façades and triggering core fears. This experience can either send us hiding behind unhealthy defense mechanisms (control, avoidance, and people-pleasing, for example) or we can stick with what's happening without judgment and find the gems of increased self-understanding and compassion. The journey of warm sisu and gentle power, therefore, requires us to soften our edges and resist becoming overly calloused from the journey.

Sisuesque is a word I use to describe the act of willfully accessing one's sisu in times of extraordinary affliction or challenge. It's the unmistakable fire in the eyes of those not bound by other people's sense of limitations, but who persist and persevere until their job is done. Whether in their daily grind or moments of extreme difficulty, sisuesque people wield their life force like an experienced bladesmith works steel to summon out the spirit and shape of an exceptional sword.

Times of transformation—such as the world-shaking volatility of the coronavirus pandemic—stir up our fears and anxieties because they challenge whatever sense of predictability and control we had over our lives. However, research shows that adversities also hold the potential to inspire purpose-driven action for the good of our personal transformation (as well as society at large) by challenging old belief structures and paving the way for new ways of thinking.[6] In other words, adversity might sometimes offer a major opportunity for us to transition to newer, healthier paradigms for ourselves and others.

CHAPTER 7:

The Three Essences of Sisu

A death blow is a blow of life to some
Who, till they died, did not alive become,
Who, had they lived, had died, but when they died,
vitality begun.

–EMILY DICKINSON[1]

I want to share with you some qualitative data on sisu I received from over one thousand people about the essence of sisu.[2] You'll find three themes that came out of this extensive analysis: sisu as extraordinary perseverance, sisu as action mindset, and sisu as embodied fortitude. Each of these offers a different angle to understanding sisu, and what unites them all is an overarching sense of moving forward no matter what—even when conditions to the contrary give us every reason not to do so.

Sisu as Extraordinary Perseverance

Sisu is what makes a person harboring a seemingly impossible dream or fighting a seemingly unbeatable adversary see past their limitations and make the most of the present moment. It's a quality that nearly everyone can point to at some point in their life. Against all odds, in a moment when—according to all logic and threat analysis—we should reasonably shrink and contract, we instead take another step and move onward into the mystery.

During my run in New Zealand, I experienced this several times a day. In one moment, I would feel completely wiped out, and yet—as if through magical intervention—I would always find a fresh wave of energy that would carry me through the stuckness and into the next moment, and then—to my continual surprise—I'd find even more available energy. The key was to just keep moving—no matter how slow. Sometimes this slowing down was indeed the key to keep moving onward and to believe that taking one step at a time would ultimately carry me where I needed to go.

The same applies to you. Whatever your situation and no matter how tough things might be, there's an energy you can tap into that's abundant, reliable, and accessible. Pay attention to any story in which the hero had to dig deep—way deeper than they knew they could dig—to find the energy and fire it took to overcome the odds. Think back to those moments in your own life to get a sense of sisu. That energy, that indomitable fire, still lives within your belly and is waiting to be unleashed.

The first of the three themes that emerged from my study—extraordinary perseverance—refers to a previously untapped capacity that becomes unlocked during periods of heightened stress, as opposed to an ability to mainly persist and stick to ordinary tasks. I'm specifically referencing perseverance during unusual trials or situations—an inner potential beyond what we assumed we had the capacity for. This means discovering energy well beyond our known boundaries of mental or physical reserves. As one of my respondents put it, "Sisu refers to the strength that lies beyond perceived limitations. Sisu exists within everyone and is usually stumbled upon when one faces insurmountable adversity." Opening to the idea that there is more strength in us than meets the eye also means gaining hope in those moments when we must travel past the edges of our known capacity.

One telling example of extraordinary perseverance comes from the world of marathon running. Whether you're an avid runner or have never put on a pair of running shoes, distance running can be an apt metaphor for almost anything in life in which we regularly *hit a wall*—a phenomenon that often happens toward the end of a marathon, where a runner's body has been depleted of its accessible reserves of glycogen. Suddenly, it feels like everything slows down, and we seem to run out of energy to finish the challenge at hand. In real life, we hit walls like this all the time. It's what happens to new parents who encounter sleep-deprivation like never before. It's what occurs to people with too many bills to pay who unexpectedly lose their job. It happens at work when you try so hard to get ahead (or break even) and the boss drops a pile of tasks on your desk on a Friday afternoon. There's just too much to handle, and our bodies respond accordingly. Finishing this book while also wrapping up my doctorate during some major life changes has been like that for me. We all have our moments like this. They're subjective, unique to each of us, and our thresholds for tolerating them tend to change over time.

The extent of our limits is way more negotiable than we know.

Extraordinary perseverance is the way that sisu shows up during these seemingly impossible moments and gets the thing done. We find a second wind and comfort our crying child; we put in the work to get a new job; we wrap up what we were in the middle of at work and set a boundary with our boss before the weekend hits. Whatever it is, our inner Gandalf stomps his staff on the precarious bridge beneath us and proclaims, *You shall not pass!* The interesting thing about the marathon analogy is that although most people who run them report hitting that seemingly unsurmountable wall toward the end of the run, end up making it across the finish line. In other words, extraordinary perseverance in this example is more the rule than an exception.

During one marathon, I'd distributed my energy reserves somewhat poorly and managed to hit the wall way earlier than normal. In fact, it happened at the ten-mile mark. I didn't even know it was possible to bonk so early in a race. But there I was—completely out of commission, in loads of pain, with sixteen miles to go. I remember my researcher brain kicking in. "How curious," it said. "I guess we'll have to take it the rest of the way entirely on sisu!" And I did. My "running" turned out to be little more than foot-shuffling for the rest of the way, but I eventually made it across the finish line that day. The experience taught me about my capacities, specifically that my reserves aren't a known quantity that's set in stone. We are almost always much stronger than we believe ourselves to be—and when we are not fixated on one true way of doing something, we can adjust our strategy. In this case, to welcome a slower pace and be more curious and less judgmental about the experience. This doesn't mean that our bodies and minds are limitless, but that the extent of our limits are way more negotiable than we know.

Six decades ago, American runner Roger Bannister became the first person to run a mile in under four minutes. Before Bannister broke that barrier, the deed had long been deemed impossible. Now, that "impossible" time has been lowered by a staggering seventeen seconds, and the four-minute mile is the standard for all male professional middle-distance runners. In fact, New Zealand's John Walker, the first man to run the mile in under 3:50, has managed to run more than one hundred sub-four-minute miles during his career.

In a 2008 study, researchers from the University of Torino in Italy found that test subjects who were informed that they were given caffeine for an energy boost (who were actually given placebos) were able to lift more weight.[3] Another team of researchers discovered a similar placebo effect in a simulated forty-kilometer timed bicycle trial.[4] The placebo effect has also been widely illustrated when it comes to pain and movement disorders.[5] There seem to be reserves of untold power within us that are just waiting to be unearthed when we need them, regardless of our previous notions regarding the scope of our abilities—and that the story we tell ourselves, or what we are told, about the situation, matters.

While triumphing against slim odds and overcoming adversity are ubiquitous in the collective narratives of human endurance, the phenomenon has been notoriously hard to explain, and only scattered research on the topic exists. Whereas perseverance is the steadfast pursuit of a task despite obstacles and discouragement, a related construct—*grit*—involves passion and its transformation into perseverance. In their 2014 paper, Angela Duckworth and James Gross (a pioneering researcher of emotion regulation based at Stanford University) indicate that one of the core components of grit is a sense of goal orientation—that is, a pursuit of a dominant life goal.[6] Although being gritty and persevering both involve continued effort despite adversities along the way, they don't necessarily require a singular adverse incident to initiate them.

The most pronounced quality of sisu involves overcoming hardship and unearthing previously unseen strength in a moment of adversity. In my data, sisu was more rarely described in relation to the pursuit of one's longstanding life goals. Sisu overlaps with certain endurance aspects of perseverance and grit, but it differs in its emphasis on short-term intensity rather than long-term stamina. Additionally, most examples of sisu in the data involve the determination and doggedness typical of grit, but without the passion or focus for an overarching life goal. Sisu is less about passion, achievement, and winning (although it can be about that too) and more about putting up a good fight and giving something everything you have. Here's another way to distinguish them: Grit and perseverance get us on the road and keep us going long. Sisu is the spare tank of fuel we tap into when we find ourselves running on empty with most of the way (for example, sixteen miles) to go before the finish line.

Sisu as Action Mindset

We humans constantly run mental simulations of our current situation and environment in order to detect opportunities and possible threats.[7] When we perceive that a current challenge is greater than our known resources, it's rational to back down—at least from the vantage point of survival. In moments like these, it's easier to be held back by our past experiences than be drawn forward by potential futures. Action mindset refers to orienting ourselves toward the future. It's an active, courageous approach to challenges that seem greater than our reserves, opportunities, and capacities. It is the mindset demonstrated by Ashley Bernardi, whom I wrote about in chapter 5, who set out on her long path of recovery from depression to ultimately upgrade her company culture and build a better life for herself and others. Anyone who's ever been bedridden for any illness or taken a chance on a big dream knows how much courage, faith, and almost divine level of audacity it takes to set on a mission to build something new.

A friend, Louis Alloro, recently called me for support during a particular rough patch in his life. Not only was he about to become a new father, but he was feeling particularly overwhelmed with an upcoming workload. I asked him if he felt any aliveness about what he was facing. His answer to me was tellingly beautiful, and it highlighted the magic of his action mindset: "No, not in this moment," he replied. "But I feel the aliveness in what's on the other side of what I am experiencing right now, and that gives me energy." Often all we need in a tight spot is one spark of hope to initiate that first action or step forward on the difficult journey ahead.

Whereas extraordinary perseverance relates to surpassing our preconceived capacities during the literal and proverbial marathons of life, action mindset is what enables us to embark on the capacity-testing journey in the first place. "It is a nondelusional fearlessness toward what would otherwise be a difficult or frightening situation," one respondent in my study wrote. Action mindset means that we consciously reach toward the edges of our perceived limits and stretch the boundaries of our psychological strength. We don't typically know how strong or capable we are until we stand face-to-face with our fears. Action mindset is an inner conviction that leans us into the headwind with faith and curiosity instead of reacting with rejection or withdrawal. Action mindset is what allowed me to dare to even dream about running across New Zealand—a challenge that would take an unbelievable amount of work for two years before the true challenge would even start! The odds were definitely against me, but what I had going for me was my action mindset. It's what got me past the initial fear where most dreams tend to stall or get buried before they've seen daylight.

There is evidence to suggest that the effect of taking action against slim odds is often more related to how we perceive challenges than the challenges themselves. Carol Dweck is a Stanford University professor of psychology who has done over three decades of research on mindset, and her team's work proposes that strength and willpower may be largely mediated by our beliefs about our abilities.[8] Of course, this could be good news or bad news—whether you believe you have sisu or not, you're correct!

Research has also found that the beliefs we hold about other people can influence how those people perform. A classic study from 1968 by Robert Rosenthal and Lenore Jacobsen revealed that the expectations teachers have of students influences their performance.[9] Elementary school students took an IQ pretest, and the teachers were later informed the names of students who were showing "unusual potential for intellectual growth." These names were randomly selected, but eight months later, Rosenthal and Jacobson discovered that the randomly selected students, who teachers were told were the most promising students, were in fact performing better. One reason for this might be that teachers paid more attention to the promising students and also expected more from them, which, in turn, encouraged those students to rise to meet the expectations. "When we expect certain behaviors of others," the researchers opined, "we are likely to act in ways that make the expected behavior more likely to occur."[10] However, another option, a related one, is that the students themselves began to view their own potential and skills in a different light.

The research of Dweck and colleagues has demonstrated that research participants who believed that their willpower was limited and fixed were more likely to give up than those who believed that their willpower was self-renewing.[11] The researchers call this *growth mindset*, meaning that we don't view our abilities as fixed but ever evolving and that we can influence them through our actions. Action mindset is a sibling to growth mindset as a quality of sisu that contributes to how we approach problems and challenges. It's signing up for that race you're not yet in shape for, putting resources into your startup even though the road ahead is exorbitantly long, finding the courage to love again after suffering a broken heart, or perhaps deciding to become a parent. A person with an action mindset climbs up a hill because they trust that on top of it awaits a clearer, wider view. They don't get too easily bogged down or overly fixated on momentary challenges; they focus on the process, on learning, and on trying until they make it.

Action mindset connects us to that eternal part of us that hopes and dares so we are not paralyzed by all that might go wrong in life. Evolution only comes before survival in the dictionary. The countless cells in our body bear witness to the triumph of natural selection and survival over millions and millions of years. We are programmed to evolve just enough to ensure survival and not to evolve any further; evolution occurs only when it's conducive to the continuity of life. For this reason, we tend to focus mostly on what's wrong simply because it has greater survival value to us. This is also referred to as *negativity bias*, which means threats will take precedence in our minds over what is lovely and good. This is why it is crucial to bring our attention to our potential, to what is working, and remind ourselves of the inner strength we have.

Sisu as a healthy reserve takes us beyond survival; it's what helps us thrive and live our purpose. Sisu enables us to fiercely tackle new challenges, tap into latent energy reserves, and harness the mental strength to carry out otherwise overwhelming tasks. Part of the power of sisu as this action mindset lies in its hope-inducing nature. It sneaks behind the myopic blur of the present moment where we can get overly focused on everything stacked against us. Action mindset is what shows us a vision of ourselves past the present hill and overwhelming mountain of work. Action mindset allows our heart a peek into our future. And if we're able to do that for even a moment, fresh air and energy flow in to rejuvenate us and remind us that we have what it takes to break free or keep going. Action mindset is about taking a leap of faith and trusting that when the moment comes, we'll be able to do what it takes, stand behind our vision, and push through the obstacles.

In research, we love to theorize where one type of strength begins and another ends, but it really doesn't matter so much in practice when we are deep in the trenches of our everyday experience. What matters is that you find the energy to get up and follow up with enough of your tasks for the day, be present for your family, be true to yourself, and ultimately, live a life that's rewarding and worthwhile. When I was running continuous marathons in New Zealand, I didn't need to contemplate which category of strength I was drawing from; it all condensed into one observation that there was something residing in me that was greater than all my pain, fear, and obstacles combined. As Albert Camus once wrote, "In the depths of winter, I finally learned that within me there lay an invincible summer."[12]

We all have an inner fire. It's that thing within us that keeps us moving on the coldest of nights. This enigmatic and hard-to-describe quality is what, to me, is the most magical and inspiring thing about us humans.

Sisu as Embodied Fortitude

For the first three years of my research into sisu, I had a nagging feeling I was missing something crucial about the topic. I couldn't quite put my finger on it, but I felt something just wasn't clicking. On New Year's Day in 2016, I was typing my research paper into the wee hours when, frustrated, I finally closed my laptop after deciding that it was no longer worth forcing it. *Whether it takes a month, year, or a decade,* I thought, *the realization will come to me when it's supposed to and not an hour earlier.* I climbed into bed and as soon as I closed my eyes, there it was.

Sisu is visceral rather than cognitive.

Two years earlier, a fellow student in the positive psychology program, Travis Millman, was reflecting on my presentation on sisu and offering some insights. While he was speaking, I noted that both of his hands were pointing firmly toward his belly. That was it! That's what I'd seen most people do during my interviews with them about sisu. I'd been so conditioned by my training in psychology that I couldn't help viewing our behavior and strength as something *mental*. The realization changed everything, and it offered me new insights about the deepest essence of sisu. Sisu wasn't like the other qualities we regularly discussed in psychology. It wasn't just about cognition, the will, or the mind.

Sure, extraordinary perseverance and action mindset are connected to our beliefs and mindsets, but sisu is more than that. Sisu is embodied. Sisu (or "intestinal fortitude" as one my respondents described it) is an entirely different animal. Sisu is visceral rather than cognitive. It's more about the responses of our body than our intellect. Peter Levine, the pioneering researcher in healing trauma, writes in his various books about what he terms *somatic intelligence*.[13] Levine and others hypothesize that the body is a vessel for intelligence whose language is more primal and visceral than our brain's. He looks at the soma as the key to healing trauma by unlocking residues of energy that have become stored in muscle cells in times of stress. The late philosopher Thomas Hanna (who coined the term *somatics* to refer to the human experience witnessed from the inside) wrote that "The state of somatic freedom is, in many ways, the optimal human state."[14] In that state, we are free from the undercurrent of locked-in trauma—not in our mind, but in our body.

Another name for intestinal fortitude is *latent power* because it lies dormant only to become available through the gateway of extraordinary challenge. In the words of Marcus Aurelius, "Remember that this which pulls the strings is the thing which is hidden within: this is the power of persuasion, this is life; this, if one may say so, is man."[15] I began to think that sisu is perhaps like an embodied equivalent of mental toughness—a power circuit that's not about physical strength per se, but instead something that resides in the soma. The engine of this particular power reserve was somehow nested inside the fibers of our body and in our very guts.

The Magic in the Belly

Why do we refer to *guts* when we talk about strength and spirit? What is it about this hidden part of our body, invisible to the bare eye, that we associate with will, courage, and resolve? The curious connection between our intestines and inner strength begins to make some sense when we take a closer look into the topic.

To start with, sisu comes from the word *sisus*, which translates as "the innermost part" or "the guts." In 1745, Finnish theologian Daniel Juslenius defined *sisucunda* as the specific location in the human body where extremely strong (and even violent affects) originate.[16] The ancient Greeks had much earlier proposed that the source of personal power lies within the intestines, and the Greco-Roman poet Persius mused, "*Magister artis ingenique largitor venter*" ("That master of the arts, that dispenser of genius, the belly").[17] Even so, after centuries of contemplation and research, the belly's full function remains a mystery to most of us. As Kousoulis notes, "Even after the first indications of its function and role appeared, every formulated idea on the nature of the gastric liquid remained open to controversy."[18]

Isn't it paradoxical that although the belly is considered the seat of strength and power in various cultures, it's the softest and most vulnerable spot on the human body? As I began my research, I discovered that the link between the gut and resilience is more than just a series of anecdotes on ancient scrolls. Recent research in gastroenterology suggests that gut microbes are part of an unconscious system that regulates our behavioral responses to stress, pain, emotions, and other people.[19] Researchers have been able to influence the brain chemistry of mice by changing the balance of bacteria in their gut, causing them to become bolder and less anxious.[20] Furthermore, transplanted gut microbiota between different strains of mice transmitted behavioral traits along with the microbiota. Recipient animals would take on traits of the donor's personality—for example, relatively timid mice would become more exploratory.[21] Recently, microbial transfer therapy in children with autism spectrum disorder (ASD) showed significant improvement in behavioral symptoms.[22]

Ecological psychology (as distinct from *ecopsychology*) is an approach based on the work of married couple J. J. Gibson and E. J. Gibson that goes beyond mainstream psychology's longstanding dichotomy between the mind and the body. Ecological psychology offers an alternative to cognitivism and behaviorism to understand how we perceive and process the world through experience.[23] It has supported developments in the cognitive sciences, where there's been a relatively recent movement that views the body as having a central role in shaping how our minds function (and therefore our actions and emotions). Some researchers aligned with this approach hypothesize that in addition to the brain, our bodies through "their perceptually guided motions through the world" contribute a great deal to our problem solving.[24]

Understanding the gut and the gut-brain connection took a big leap forward with the discovery of the enteric nervous system (ENS) in the middle of the nineteenth century. Because of its complexity, size, and similarity to the central nervous system (CNS), the enteric nervous system is described not only as the "brain in the gut" but our original brain.[25] All of this new research is still finding its feet, but it brings up some stirring ideas regarding our understanding of mind-body integration.

A psychologist friend once pointed to her toddler and said, "Isn't it just fascinating how if a baby is uneasy and crying, we immediately check if she's slept enough, if she needs to eat, or if she needs her diaper changed? If it's an adult who's unwell, we send them to therapy!" It's not so much like that when we grow up. As adults, we're governed by the world of thinking and abstraction, and the body's role in mental health and well-being becomes largely forgotten. Could the secret to finding strength amid life's trials, ever-present transformations, and even trauma be found in the somatic side of the human experience? What if we looked immediately to our breath, sleep, nutrition, and physical movement?

CHAPTER 8:

The Shadow of Sisu

*Your hand opens and closes, opens and closes. If it were always
a fist or always stretched open, you would be paralyzed. Your
deepest presence is in every small contracting and expanding, the
two as beautifully balanced and coordinated as birds' wings.*

–RUMI[1]

My research also revealed something startling: too much sisu (or sisu of the unhealthy sort) can lead to destructive outcomes. Examples include the obsession of one task at the expense of others, ignoring other people's perspectives, failing to sympathize with their struggles, and acting toward other people in ways that erode trust, safety, and connection. So, while sisu and qualities like determination, grit, and mental toughness push us forward and help us get stuff done, they're not foolproof. In fact, without the right balance of these qualities, we can become lost in the perceived importance of our mission, harm ourselves and others, or put even more obstacles in our way.

Unhealthy expressions of sisu are widely tolerated and even glorified. Prioritizing work over family for self-serving goals, skipping self-care, being harsh toward those who don't seem to be working as hard as we do, and constantly putting our own needs first are examples of shadow sisu. Unfortunately, it's devastating to personal harmony, interpersonal safety, and our collective well-being. Endless striving and the acquisition mindset invariably lead to division, disconnection, and even merciless-ness. Scott Barry Kaufman, the author of *Transcend: The New Science of Self-Actualization*, describes a healthy personality from the point of view of humanistic psychology as "one that constantly moves toward freedom, responsibility, self-awareness, meaning, commitment, personal growth, maturity, integration, and change, rather than . . . status, achievement, or even happiness."[2] It makes sense: when we prioritize constant profit-making or focus predominantly on ourself at the expense of everything else, it's bound to affect how we treat each other and the planet. For this reason, any exploration into sisu must include an effort to ensure that one's sisu is a healthy resource, as opposed to a detriment to oneself and others.

What Sisyphus Knew

In the Ancient Greek myth, Sisyphus was doomed by Zeus to push a heavy boulder up a steep hill forever. The task was eternally futile—every time Sisyphus approached the top of the hill, the boulder would roll back down to the bottom, and he would have to start all over again. Sometimes we find ourselves in a rut like that, as if all we can do is keep hitting our head against the wall. Maybe we're just blind to the habits that brought us to a bad spot, but sometimes we know that we aren't helping ourselves, and we keep doing what we're doing anyway. The mythical Sisyphus was in a choiceless situation, but his story still has something to say about stubborn power and how it can lead to repetitive, harmful, or depleting patterns.

Most of us don't have jobs as physically demanding and hopeless as Sisyphus's, but we're still expected to work on grueling tasks for long hours at the ongoing expense of our physical and mental health—not to mention our sense of meaning and purpose—simply because that's what the job demands, and the system we're a part of applies constant pressure on us to remain on the hamster wheel. It can take everything we've got just to step back for a moment, take a break, and evaluate the craziness of our situation. And it often takes a whole lot more than that to stand up to the power that seems to keep us pushing that boulder up the hill.

Based on the results of my survey, I found three categories of harmful sisu: sisu that's harmful to the individual, sisu that's harmful to others, and sisu that impairs our ability to think and reason. I'll dive into each of them below. To examine your own sisu in relation to some particular task you might be facing, I invite you to ask yourself if any of them sound familiar.

Sisu That's Harmful to the Individual

This category relates to the negative physical and mental health consequences of constantly overextending ourselves. Taking prolonged or unreasonable risks in life, for example, can lead to more accidents, injuries, burnout, and even death. Or we might instead take on more responsibility than we can bear or make foolish or unsensible sacrifices. One respondent of my survey also noted that having unrealistic assumptions about our mental or physical reserves can lead to foolhardiness, depletion, and backlash. Although public discourse seems to glorify mental strength and perpetuates the push-through-at-all-costs mentality, the sisu of gentle power invites us to look into our unhelpful patterns with honest discernment, curiosity, and compassion.

"It is hard to see the label when you're inside the jar," a friend of mine once said. The tricky part in this discussion is that we typically don't know what we don't know. For this reason, a practice of self-understanding is critical. In my personal experience, there's always something we don't know about ourselves—at least not well—and our process for making decisions is often a mystery. The path of self-inquiry isn't easy, either. It can prove painful to uncover those things we've hidden from ourselves for years and years, or perhaps an entire lifetime. It's that honest inquiry with ourselves, however, that moves us toward more freedom and gentle power.

When I came up with the idea to run across New Zealand, I found lots of good reasons to do so—and they all made my crazy endeavor sound a bit more logical. I needed to do research for my doctoral dissertation, for example, and it was also a great opportunity to launch the Sisu Not Silence campaign. But I also wanted to do it because there were questions I had about myself that I didn't know the answers to. I needed to find out who I was in terms of my inner strength, alone, day after day, when there was nothing to distract myself with other than the passing scenery on the road. In short, I needed to be with just me and my sisu.

Through inner work and self-knowledge,
we have the opportunity to change
our patterns at any moment.

On one particular morning during the run, the road was unusually silent. It felt as if it were holding its breath as I trotted along under the burning Aotearoa sun with my blistered feet and aching ankle (not to mention aching back, thighs, butt, and calves). There was a sense of approaching breakdown in the air, and I realized that I'd let the run run me down. Instead of owning the run I'd envisioned and organized, the run was owning me. I'd defaulted to my perfectionism and habitual sense of obligation, making harmony and alignment take a back seat, and I was in danger of harming myself. But I've also learned that breakdowns are often followed by breakthroughs. Then suddenly, there it was: I understood more clearly than I'd ever understood before that I always chose to do the hard thing rather than what was easy, and I rarely practiced gentleness with myself. Paradoxically, being gentle with myself was way tougher than, say, running several ultramarathons in a row.

For two years, I'd trained myself to be comfortable running tens of miles per day. At the end of my preparation, running a marathon felt like a solid warmup. But I was doing something nearly impossible now, which meant approaching a checkpoint of reality. The flashes of pain that spiked up my right ankle were getting more frequent and sharp. I was running the options over in my mind: quit, take a break, or push through it? How was I supposed to know what the ultimate limit was? What if I gave up too soon because I felt done in the moment? What if I felt differently tomorrow and my body was fine after all?

Through self-reflection and discernment, we have the opportunity to change our patterns at any moment. While my run might seem like an unusually extreme example, I think most of us go through similar struggles and doubt. I know I'm not alone in defaulting to taking the hard way out, as opposed to what comes more natural or easy. Even now, at times I'm drawn to bypass the quiet request from my body to get enough sleep or to ask for support from my family and friends in tough times. I can also hesitate to request an extension for a deadline when I'm overworked, or I can be tempted to say *yes* to a request or proposal that doesn't feel aligned and thus ignore invitations to slow down and honor myself. Even now, I sometimes turn away from balance and harmony, but I'm learning.

Sisu That's Harmful to Others

Most of us love witnessing extreme people do extreme things, and we welcome tales of superhuman feats that remind us that life doesn't have to be boring, normal, or mediocre. They remind us that there is greatness inside us. We don't typically think about what those people had to sacrifice in order to accomplish such things or how their sacrifices impacted other people. Sisu can help us attain the seemingly unattainable, but it can also encourage us to lose sight of what else is important in life. Just think of all the families—supportive spouses and admiring children—who were sacrificed at the altar of wealth, success, or mere self-validation. That's what can happen when you constantly prioritize self-focused goals over presence, connection, and love.

In my data, some respondents expressed concern that individuals with too much sisu can be merciless, unfeeling, or unable to attune to the needs of their families and colleagues. For example, one person in the survey noted, "A person with sisu is someone who is trustworthy and seeks to make it on their own at all times. They are not necessarily the most helpful person because they think everyone else is capable of making it if they only bother to try and have the will." Another highlighted arrogance and aggression as hallmarks of people with too much sisu. They can be "bullying. Overly critical of others. Too much [sisu] makes a person intimidating to others, thus cultivating disrespect amongst peers. A person possessing sisu must also possess grace and kindness. It is a fine line to walk."

In an organizational setting, these noted detriments can wreak havoc. When it comes to toxic leadership, disruptive patterns are often rooted in the leader's own sense of incompetence, which they try to hide by overcompensating through behaviors that create an image of high performance. In turn, this false picture is glorified and validated. Since we tend to praise superhuman qualities ("Can you believe they put in ninety hours of work last week? Look at that commitment!"), we can easily miss the signs of unhealthy sisu, but there's one surefire way to find out: over time, we simply feel depleted and running short when we're exposed to these people (unless we're swayed by the same need for speed and achievement, of course).

A friend recently told me about his dad, an acclaimed entrepreneur and endurance athlete. Growing up, he would always praise my friend for his accomplishments but showed very little empathy when he didn't excel. It's sometimes difficult to understand or even pick up on the needs and distress of others, particularly when we're so taken in by our own gifts and displays of excellence. My friend said he consistently felt like he wasn't making the cut in life and was never quite good enough for his father. Whether this was true on his father's side or not, my friend ultimately decided to limit his interactions with him. This created some hard feelings in the family, but my friend was also gradually able to become more self-confident and relaxed.

Ilmari Määttänen and Pentti Henttonen (with the help of psychologist Julius Väliaho) at the University of Helsinki conducted a series of studies to develop the first ever self-evaluation scale to measure one's sisu. The study validates the findings that sisu can either be harmful or helpful. Currently their team is researching sisu in the context of work life to create real-life applications for it. The findings outline a connection between healthy sisu and individual well-being, but they also propose a steady correlation with unhealthy sisu and work-related stress.[3] Again, sisu is a fantastic tool to use for our goals, but we must learn to use it well.

Sisu That Impairs Our Ability to Think and Reason

Too much sisu can cloud our minds and leads to results quite other than those we initially intended. Impaired reasoning is one of these results, and its role as an agent of *shadow sisu* was centrally represented in the survey data. It's also useful to highlight this type of harmful sisu because it helps explain why sisu can generate such detrimental effects on people and those close to them. Ultimately, it's our quality of thought that underpins all forms of sisu from the harmful to the healthy.

If I had kept running just one more day in New Zealand, I might not have been able to salvage much from the endeavor. At some point—mostly without our awareness—our tendency to take *one more step* crosses over into a point of no return to become *one more step too far.* In a culture that's addicted to overachievement, there's always one more step, one more task, one more challenge, one more seemingly impossible goal to strive for. Far too many of us are hardwired to push it to the extreme.

There's a saying I once heard: "The trouble with humans is that we don't know how to get started, and then we don't know when to stop." That's why we can remain so fixated on a certain direction, even when it's clear that the direction is leading us away from what's most important (or, as I sometimes put it, "There's a fine line between a badass and a dumbass"). Too much sisu of the latter sort can lead us to lose track of the big picture, misjudge our capacities, and hesitate to ask for help. As one of my survey respondents put it, "You need to focus clearly on what you are now, but you also need to be able to learn from the past and be creative in finding new solutions when you seem to be stuck." Unlike Sisyphus, who was cursed to eternal boulder-pushing by Zeus, we have the capacity to question if we're doing something difficult just because we're accustomed to living that way. A successful entrepreneur I know once confessed to me that if something important didn't feel "hard" and if she didn't feel like she was sacrificing to attain it, she always ended up questioning her effort no matter how well she did.

Healthy sisu requires the ability to pause and look at the boulders we are pushing. To what extent are we doing something hard just because we are used to doing it, because we once, under totally different circumstances, decided that this is the path, or because we see other people doing the same? Just like Sisyphus was doomed to his task by an external authority, we may be pushing along our path under a set of expectations imposed on us from outside. We all live inside the bubble of our zeitgeist. Move us into a different time, era, or community or have us raised by different parents, and that which we deem important, outlandish, and desirable immediately changes. Currently, our collective discourse is tilted toward effort over balance, hard over soft, reason over love, and performance over presence. However, the good news is that culture is a set of rules collectively accepted by a group of people. These rules were created by us, and that means they can be changed by us. In our reality, there is no Hades with a smoking fork waiting to punish you if you choose to quit the race, change your mind about something you were gung ho about, and prioritize more self-care. If anything, there is a delighted sisu researcher, me, who will nod with relief and gratitude for the excellent example you're setting by cutting yourself some slack when it's needed.

The path out of these harmful forms of sisu travels through the clarifying fields of self-awareness. Awareness takes what was hidden in our subconscious or unconscious mind and reveals our patterns so we can make more informed decisions going forward. Just as on that transformational day in New Zealand when I realized that for most of my life, I'd believed that things were supposed to be tough. I also thought that if I didn't show how hard I was trying, I wasn't playing my part well enough. But it wasn't true. I realized I had the power to end my suffering by making different choices, but I couldn't do that until I realized there were different choices I could make.

During my run in New Zealand (and all the accompanying challenges I imposed on myself to study inner strength), I found that once I burned through my old pattern of hard sisu and pushed through hardship with sheer determination, I was surprised to find it replaced by something much more steady, organic, and deep. This other power circuit felt more embodied than intellectual and seemed to have less to do with sheer mental resolve. In fact, it felt more like surrender. This was the personal discovery that brought me to think of sisu in an entirely different way. Maybe it was way more about gentleness than I'd known.

There will always be more roads to run, more hills to climb, and more boulders to push around. The point here isn't to run away from hard things as they will help us evolve and discover parts of ourselves. But we can face those difficulties with less force and stubbornness, choosing instead to greet them with more acceptance and litheness whenever possible. We can all learn to navigate both our strength and fragility with care. When we are ready, it takes one moment of clarity and courage to step on the path of gentle power, and our life changes.

PART IV

The Nature of Gentle Power

Know the Tough, Live from the Soft

Seeing the insignificant speaks of insight.
Maintaining softness speaks of strength.

–LAO TZU[1]

My body flew across the air like some kind of white, oversized scarf as my aikido teacher and I practiced. He was gently pushing me to the edge of my skills by not being too careful or too hard; instead, he trusted me to hold my own. I've always loved aikido because of its emphasis on becoming more loving and caring. In practice, this means that your full presence is also on your training partner, and you maintain precise awareness of how much pressure you are using through your points of contact with them. You only use as much as is necessary.

It's a fine line to walk. When a beginner starts training in aikido, their grip is often either too hard and rigid (which blocks the flow of movement) or too soft and loose (which loses the connection). An aikido teacher I met in Malaysia told me that one's grip begins *before* the hands even touch. "Your grip is decided before there is a contact," he said. "It comes from your intention. The grip on your partner is just the visible manifestation of your inner grip."

As in aikido, learning to interact with others through both power and gentleness, and grace and strength, is a lifelong journey. And because everyone's energy is different, we must know ourselves thoroughly and maintain pristine awareness in every connection we make in the dojo of life.

Power and Force

Esther Hillesum was a Dutch Jewish activist and mystic who was killed in Auschwitz when she was twenty-nine. In her diary, she famously wrote, "There is a difference between being hardy and being hard."[2] Sisu is like that too. Sisu combined with gentleness leads to power that is unforced, tender, and tempered. Hillesum's life was an epitome of gentle power over force. During the Nazi occupation and genocide, she retained her joy for life, and her lucid intelligence and sympathy were themselves a form of resistance. There are few things more formidable than this. Gentle power is adaptable, accepting, patient, and honest. And because it doesn't wear masks, it has very little to lose. You can't steal from someone who isn't concerned about possessions, and you can't hurt someone who has learned to sit equally well with their love and pain. For that person, nothing is worth sacrificing the peace of mind that comes from such inner alignment.

After the publication of *Het Verstoorde Leven [An Interrupted Life]* in 1981, scholars around the world displayed interest in the Hillesum's writings. Anna Aluffi Pentinini, whose work focuses on education and pedagogy, introduces Hillesum's distinction between the "hardy but not hard" as an essential maxim for education of social professionals.[3] Knowing how to be hardy without being too hard requires a level of self-awareness and a particular set of skills that are rarely discussed, let alone taught. Being a leader who models gentle power in this way—be it as a parent, friend, coworker, lover, or neighbor—means learning how to integrate and harmonize the soft and the solid. It means to know what our intentions are before we manifest our grip so we activate our power gracefully without forcing it upon others. It means to commit ourselves to the journey of being fully human.

One day in the middle of my research on sisu, I was taking a break from work to watch my foster puppy play with a dog that was at least three times her size. While playing rather rambunctiously, they were both remarkably careful with each other, especially with their sharp teeth. Their play, while primal and wild, also demonstrated the ability of living beings to control their power with very little effort and follow within rules of trust, care, and respect.

We all encounter moments like this. Even though we're conditioned to think of gentleness as weakness, examples of gentle power are everywhere around us. We see it in the way that water carves away at the hardest substances over time. We see it in the stately silence of powerful trees whose brawny roots conceal the true secret to their strength. We see it in fierce animals nurturing their young. We see it in our partners, our parents, our children.

I also think of gentle power as *graceful strength*. It's a more refined version of determination and fortitude. Gentle power moves the needle from winning, achievement, and status to well-being, maturity, and personal growth. Gentle power isn't just perseverance, sisu, and grit; it asks us to keep in mind what these qualities are for. Gentle power, to me, has an unimposing but robust feel to it—the kind that leaves a soft but tantalizing sensation in the bottom of my belly. Like an irresistible dream, it encourages me forward, promising something kinder and better. Gentle power doesn't grasp, doesn't impose, doesn't demand, doesn't pretend, and yet, it expresses, states, and excels.

David Hawkins notes that "Power gives life and energy; force takes these away."[4] Power resides within us, whereas force is what we impose upon others. Force divides and disconnects, whereas power joins, nourishes, accompanies, and literally empowers others. Power is still and self-assured; force is coercive and usually results in counterforce and pushback. Most of us can easily mistake force for power, if only because we continually receive messages from the world that force is the same as strength.

We can enhance our *power* by developing our capacities for integrity, compassion, and systems intelligence (described later, in part 5 of the book) and by thinking about the long-term and broad-spectrum implications of our actions, thoughts, and beliefs. Every action we commit results in a multitude of effects, some that can last years and even decades. This journey is different for each person. At different times in our lives, we might need to work on opposite ends of the gentle power spectrum—focusing on power at times and sometimes addressing our gentleness.

Whatever you're working on in a given moment, gentle power involves harmony and a just-so grip. To restate the Comte-Sponville quote from chapter 4, "Gentleness is gentleness only as long it owes nothing to fear." When we act out of fear, we're usually either defending ourselves or trying to maintain some grasp over an idea, desire, or person. The opposite of fear isn't bravery or love, but *letting go*. So much of the work of leading with gentle power involves letting go, accepting the situation or person before us, and ensuring that our expressions of power aren't manifesting in the world as expressions of force.

Love Is the Way

I've been drawn to Eastern philosophy and practices for nearly half of my life, which led me to explore different martial arts with various teachers around the world. One of my most significant lessons about sisu and gentle power involved martial arts and the application of yin energy: the most powerful strikes come from a soft and pliable body. Suppleness and relaxation beat hardness and stiffness any time.

Gentle power isn't altogether different from the Taoist belief that the polarities of hard and soft, resistance and surrender, hot and cold, loud and quiet, intellect and intuition, and so on work best when they harmonize together. When this occurs at an advanced and impeccable level, some would refer to this harmony as *knowing what is* or the cessation of suffering. Although it isn't the same as *enlightenment* in the Eastern sense of the term, in Western terminology this *knowing what is* could be reflected in the heightened psychological states such as peak experience, flow, and self-actualization. In my experience, the harmonious integration of the hard and the soft, the yang and the yin, can be practiced through knowing our power (including its shadow manifestations of powerlessness on one side and abuse of power on the other) and gentleness (including its shadows of boundarilessness and meekness) and bringing the two into harmony.

Power without love is reckless and abusive,
and love without power is sentimental
and anemic. —Martin Luther King Jr.

Aikido was developed by its founder (Morihei Ueshiba or "O'Sensei") to be a path to integrate these energies in order to embody and share true peace.[5] Other martial arts share similar intentions, particularly those influenced by Taoism. As Lao Tzu writes:

> Man at his birth is supple and weak; at his death, firm and strong. (So it is with) all things. Trees and plants, in their early growth, are soft and brittle; at their death, dry and withered. Thus it is that firmness and strength are the concomitants of death; softness and weakness, the concomitants of life. Hence he who (relies on) the strength of his forces does not conquer; and a tree which is strong will fill the outstretched arms, (and thereby invites the feller.) Therefore the place of what is firm and strong is below, and that of what is soft and weak is above.[6]

Applying this same approach to today's organizational and business arena would mean a radical shift in priorities, namely putting more emphasis on the development of virtues and character and less on profit and ruthless strategy. It would mean prioritizing being human first and a businessperson (or capitalist businessperson) second. In business, when power arises as a topic of discussion, it's usually about how to attain more of it. Power gets reduced to yet another tool for self-oriented achievement.

Leaders would do better to ask how power—and what kind of power—encourages us to become more wise, balanced, wholesome, and caring. We need to realize, as Martin Luther King Jr. famously expressed, that "Power without love is reckless and abusive, and love without power is sentimental and anemic. Power at its best is love."[7] And if character is a skill that we can learn and cultivate, perhaps love is too. Maybe love doesn't have to be some abstract, elusive thing that we wish we had more of, but something concrete and tangible we can *practice*, just as a martial artist practices their techniques and forms along the path to mastery.

Barbara Fredrickson (whose work I mentioned in chapter 5) has a further take on love, which is that love—"felt in the context of a safe, close relationship"—is the circulation of renewed interest within an endless cycle of revealing new aspects of oneself and the other.[8] In other words, love is a devotional practice that develops over time. O'Sensei also taught that "the true meaning of the term 'samurai' is one who serves and adheres to the power of love," and that aikido's purpose is about creating and reconciling the human family.[9] In his writings about the way of the samurai and Bushido (the ethical values and moral code of conduct of the samurai), Daniele Bolelli notes, "When a samurai loses balance, strength turns into stiffness and Bushido turns into a prison."[10] Just as the *Tao* encourages us to become more harmonious and loving, gentle power is rooted in our ability to embody love, care, and forgiveness—toward others, and also ourselves. "Ultimately, we have just one moral duty: To reclaim large areas of peace in ourselves. More and more peace and reflect it towards others. And the more peace there is in us, the more peace there will also be in our troubled world," Etty Hillesum concluded in her diaries written between 1941 and October 1942 while living in Nazi occupied Amsterdam and later at concentration camps.[11]

Sisu, Gentle Power, and the Path Forward

The principles of gentle power, with sisu at their core, apply to all of us because they relate to our ability to find balance and harmony in the middle of life's challenges. Sisu complements the much-spoken Scandinavian lifestyle concepts of lagom and hygge with its unique cultural connotations of strength as a quality of integrity and character. And through the frame of gentle power, sisu is also connected to the yin and yang of Taoism, as well as the business-world's conversation around "soft" and "tough" skills. Balanced sisu also speaks to the inner fortitude pursued by certain martial artists. Only when sisu is mediated by the supple strength of gentleness does our connection to inner power come completely online. Furthermore, sisu is essential to gentle power because it fortifies our striving for better ways to be who we are and to do what we do.

The next frontier, as I see it, requires us to emphasize gentleness in a way that recognizes its inherent strength and vital role in all interaction from the interpersonal to the broader systems of society. It's time to open up the dialogue about strength well beyond the already-known issue of *what is there to be done* so we take a closer and more honest look at *how we do* what we do. The way we do things with sisu that is balanced and harmonious is with grace, compassion, and as much steadfastness and courage as we can muster. Indomitable resolve combined with gentleness and personal responsibility lead to true power—a kind of tempered strength. This is what the future of leadership will be made of. Why? Because by now we have tried pretty much everything else, and we have failed. It is time to make gentle power our North Star.

CHAPTER 10

Self-Worth

Who looks outside dreams; who looks inside awakes.

—CARL JUNG[1]

Self-worth is essentially all about self-respect and our sense of personal value. Because self-worth helps us set and maintain boundaries as well as view ourselves as deserving of love and dignity, it also comes into play in every encounter we have with others. Self-worth is the most important tool for the evolution of the self because it implies healthy self-reliance and independence. That means that we aren't overly swayed by what others think or feel about us and that we favor equitable relationships over psychological entanglements that do none of the involved parties any lasting good.

If I'd had self-worth figured out earlier in my life, I would've paid more attention to the red flags signaling that my partnership was abusive. I wouldn't have explained away the warning signs and overstayed in the name of somebody else's recovery. I also would've accepted some different work opportunities that I felt too inferior to say yes to, and I would've been able to relax more in relationships that were safe and nurturing because I would've trusted that my boundaries were intact and functioning.

The closest word to self-worth in Finnish is *omanarvontunto*. Like sisu, omanarvontunto is one of those words that doesn't have close counterparts in other languages. The end of the word (*tunto*) means "to feel and acknowledge," so self-worth in Finnish has this essential component of self-knowledge, like the "Know thyself" maxim that was popular among Greek philosophers.

A Fine Line Between Nice and Kind

In a world that presents contradictory messages regarding kindness, compassion, softness, and vulnerability, it can be hard to know where to draw the line and hold boundaries with others sometimes. Creating communities and forming bonds require us to show up for each other and occasionally make sacrifices. When setting boundaries and expressing our needs, we might regularly encounter pushback from others, but not doing so endangers our sovereignty and puts us at risk of losing our sense of direction. On top of that, it's easy to err on the side of rigidity and harshness when we're first learning how to make boundaries with others. Just as in the martial arts example I gave earlier, it takes a lot of dedicated training to learn to adjust the firmness of our grip to fit each partner and situation.

Figuring out how to balance strength and suppleness has been one of the biggest challenges of my life. Ultimately, I realized that prioritizing balance (while a noble goal) made me feel like I was constantly walking a tightrope from which I could fall at any moment. It was simply too much pressure. I have since learned to embrace the idea of harmony instead. It allows me to blend with each moment with more ease and less fear of failure.

With practice, expressing our boundaries with grace and harmony becomes increasingly embodied, natural, and relaxed. It's like when we first learn to drive—at first, our braking is jerky and abrupt, and it takes lots of repetitions to get the subtle motions ingrained in our body. If we understood that learning how to do this was going to take a while from the outset, we could enjoy the process with a lot more acceptance and compassion— not to mention we'd make learning it mandatory like driving school!

I mentioned Rick Smith and inner authority in chapters 1 and 4. As a reminder, inner authority means to sit with the charge of something uncomfortable without closing off from the hard feelings it entails. In addition to being a senior trainer of Authentic Relating, Rick has written two books on leadership, and he has facilitated his own workshops, seminars, and retreats for over ten years for what he calls *awakened leadership*.

I met Rick over lunch in a small town on the west coast of Bali. In our interview, I told him about a situation in my past in which I struggled to express a boundary with a friend. In a healthy relationship, requesting to reestablish more balance or communicating changed priorities is usually straightforward. Unfortunately, in the example I discussed with Rick, my requests triggered extraordinary pushback in the form of guilt-tripping and manipulation. The experience was hard on me, but invaluable. It helped expose a wound I was still carrying about my sense of self-worth that was related to my need for others to view me as loving and kind no matter what. Because of this wound, it was difficult for me to express a firm no, and I ended up overextending myself way beyond what was okay. This not only made me the recipient of my friend's unprocessed emotional baggage but contributed to the situation becoming much more entangled than it really needed to be.

I had adopted a behavioral strategy to ensure that I was perceived as harmless and that would encourage people to be nice to me in return. Unfortunately, doing so meant forgetting my boundaries and self-worth and instead forming an identity whose sense of safety depended on meeting the assumed needs of the people I met. Don't get me wrong—the world needs us to be friendly and loving, but when it becomes a fixed priority or an expectation at the expense of our self-worth, we actually become the problem. We not only become a target for others, but we're also living dishonestly with ourselves. And we're perpetuating unhealthy patterns that ultimately cause suffering and unhappiness for everyone.

"There is a big difference between *kind* and *nice*," Rick told me. *Nice*, he elaborated, is what you do to get people to like you; it's focused on what you think people want and adhering to that to get what you yearn to receive from them. In its root is fear. *Kind*, on the other hand, is about what is actually needed in a situation. Telling the difference between the two can sometimes be difficult. Rick continued to explain that when we are nice, we are giving away our power to the other person. Their potential disapproval can hold us hostage. When we are kind, we are empowering ourselves, as we are not basing our success on what others think of us. Rick also talks about the *tender edge*, the sweet and often uncomfortable space between safety and risk, where our comfort zone expands and growth happens. It is when you lean into the discomfort of letting someone down in order to be true to yourself. It's a moment of vulnerability in which you "pulse between safety and risk," as he describes it.

The situation I'd described to Rick had completely exhausted me. I'd experienced violent abuse from someone close to me before, so it was nearly unthinkable for me to choose to challenge someone else. I regularly chose appeasement and to override my needs so I didn't have to feel the pain. What's more, because I'd experienced the trauma of abuse, I feared doing anything that might cause discomfort to someone else. It took me the longest time to be willing to sit with all of that and not close off from the psychological tension and pain.

The Courage to Disappoint

Oriah Mountaindreamer writes, "I want to know if you can disappoint another to be true to yourself; if you can bear the accusation of betrayal and not betray your soul; if you can be faithless and therefore trustworthy?"[2] That quote once helped me to process some guilt I had over leaving a long-term relationship, which was one of the hardest things I've ever done. I was eventually able to make my way through the pain and doubt, and ultimately, the new path led to growth for both of us in ways that we would not have been able to attain by staying together. In fact, two years after our separation, my former partner thanked me for seeing things as they were and for having the courage to be honest.

Honesty—either with ourselves or others—is often the hardest thing to do. Honesty can feel like a scary leap into the unknown when all we can do is freefall and trust that there's a method somewhere in the madness. Every time I do it, I have to remind myself how it's been worth it in the past and that there's undeniable value in taking the risk and communicating with as much love and clarity as I can.

> Honesty—when delivered with kind
> consideration—naturally builds more intimacy.

When it comes to the organizational domain, if we're not able to bear the emotional discomfort of feeling like we've sometimes let other people down, our compass becomes compromised, we lose our inner authority, and we can't be trusted to make informed decisions for the good of the whole. Dedicating ourselves to the path of gentle power, however, can help us identify those aspects of ourselves that compromise the bigger picture for a temporary sense of safety (or seeking approval). As Benjamin Franklin is credited with saying nearly three hundred years ago, "An ounce of prevention is worth a pound of cure." If we choose to stay open and learn from all of our experiences, from work to family life, we can develop greater discernment and insight in our leadership as well and, over time, become excellent at creating something sound and mutually beneficial from the foundation.

In most of my relationships, I've been able to express my need for realignment, find common ground, and ultimately grow closer to other people as a result. The same will most likely be the case for you most of the time. In healthy relationships, honesty—when delivered with consideration—naturally builds more intimacy. Everyone involved steps further into the preciousness and courage of revealing their true experience instead of holding back out of fear or pride. And sometimes it takes this degree of honesty to successfully transform the relationship into something else—a close friendship instead of a romantic partnership, for example, or occasional partners in business as opposed to regular collaborators. Whatever happens, welcome it as a natural part of life. If nothing else, honesty and directness are chances to honor yourself and others as long as you accept that change is inevitable and that it's okay to loosen your grasp on it all (especially on people). Each of us must travel our own path, and part of self-worth is following its course no matter where it takes us.

CHAPTER 11

Gentle Power and Society

We think too much and feel too little. More than machinery we need humanity. More than cleverness, we need kindness and gentleness. Without these qualities life will be violent, and all will be lost.

–CHARLIE CHAPLIN[1]

T his crucial time in history has been labeled the *digital revolution*, which many consider to be the beginning of the *information age*. Our period is marked by the rapid evolution of technologies, associated shifts in human communication, and growing concern regarding impending crises in the environmental, financial, and political realms. Although turbulent times like these can feel scary and disruptive, they're also transition points of fundamental change. Sometimes it takes getting yanked out of our business-as-usual trance for us to seek new perspectives and solutions.

The Field of Gentle Power

Nicholas Christakis stepped onto the stage of the University of Pennsylvania auditorium in front of a room full of applied positive psychology master's students and graduates at their annual summit. Christakis was one of the keynote speakers I was most interested in. He's the Sterling professor of social and natural science at Yale University, where he also directs the Human Nature Lab. His work focuses on the socioeconomic, biosocial, and evolutionary determinants of behavior, health, and longevity. Together with Ray Fowler at Harvard University, Christakis set out to study whether happiness can spread from person to person and whether niches of happiness form within social networks. On the day in question, Christakis was going to speak about contagion theory.

Contagion theory suggests that just as a virus spreads through infection and contamination, certain aspects of our emotional and cognitive realms can be transferred from person to person.[2] Although the fact that certain things, like depression and addiction, spread through social networks might seem intuitive, the surprisingly good news is that positive emotions (like happiness, for example) are contagious in exactly the same way. This was a groundbreaking discovery for me. And it doubled down my interest in cultivating healthy attitudes in order to benefit others in my inner and outer circles.

We consciously engineer gentle power in our own lives in order to spread it to others.

Later that same year, I attended a lecture delivered by Karen Reivich—a determined and energetic researcher who was presenting on her substantial work on resilience. Karen asked us to describe a moment from childhood when we felt seen and cared for. Most of us raised our hands, and some of us shared examples. I talked about Maija Oksala, my first-grade teacher in Seinäjoki, the small city where I grew up. Maija had loving brown eyes, a heart of gold, and a smile that always felt welcoming. Just remembering all that warms my heart three decades later! As I listened to my fellow students speak, I couldn't help but notice the varied nature of their stories: a teacher had helped one learn to read, a neighbor taught one to ride a bicycle when their single-parenting mother didn't have the time, a smile from a stranger from across the street. All these experiences left lasting positive imprints, but I was struck with how random they were—they were occasional, instead of systemic.

Hearing these stories reminded me of Christakis's keynote speech, and I began to wonder how we could make events and gestures like these more dependable and regular. Stumbling across encouragement and kindness is great, but what if more of our workplaces, family lives, and social domains were engineered with more contagious goodness in mind? I experimented with an online endeavor to create virtuous systems in society through daily micro-actions, but nothing much came of it. Even so, writing this book a decade later, I'm still convinced it can be done. Through small individual efforts, it's possible to create containers for gentle-powered leadership and spread that to create entire cultures that are grounded in well-being and goodness. This means more self-actualization, happiness, and creativity on the individual level, and better decision-making, policy creation, and equity on the global level. Ideally, we consciously engineer gentle power in our own lives in order to spread it to others.

Sisu and gentle power aren't just qualities that live in individuals. They arise, evolve, and spread when conditions are right in the multidimensional field of our interactions. As I covered earlier in the book, the benefits of psychological safety (Amy Edmondson's work), positive emotions (Barbara Fredrickson), and high-quality connections (Jane Dutton) are undeniable, and Christakis and Fowler's research further demonstrates that we can leverage these positive ingredients to generate benefits on the larger scale. Creating cultures of psychological safety and well-being isn't just good for us; they're necessary components for our collective evolution.

There's No Miracle Drug

Some years ago, I was working in Silicon Valley with two other cofounders to develop an app that would help people in developing countries monetize their knowledge. A great deal of money is made by large market research companies that connect researchers to interviewees, but the interviewees earn very minimal compensation. Our endeavor came out of the Global Solutions Program at Singularity University, founded by tech entrepreneur Peter Diamandis and Google's head futurist, Ray Kurtzweil. They promote the idea that exponential technology should be used not only for business gain but also to solve humanity's greatest challenges—climate disruption, global illness, hunger, poverty, and so on. Exponential technology according to them offers the potential to democratize knowledge, opportunity, and resources, and addresses potential ways to help everyone on a global scale.

I'd learned about all of this while attending the Singularity University Global Solutions Program with about eighty other students. I was surrounded in that brightly lit classroom by a sea of social entrepreneurs, MDs, an actual rocket scientist, social innovators, futurists, computer scientists, and others who all looked focused, smart, and—like me—self-conscious. We were all also quite serious about "making the world a better place" through the Holy Grail of exponential technology—an umbrella term for modern tech that follows Moore's law (which dictates that the number of transistors in a chip doubles every two years, which in turn means that computer processing speed doubles about every couple of years). All of us in that room had been selected from several thousand applicants, and all of us were aiming to produce an original idea that took advantage of exponential technology to address one of humanity's grand challenges and positively impact the lives of at least one million people in just a matter of years.

During the nearly two-month long program, in a matter of some weeks, all of us studied, listened to lectures, ate, and slept (although most of us not long or well) on NASA Ames Research Park campus in Mountain View, California, where the program took place, staying in the same dorms as astronaut trainees would. During the first couple of weeks, the cream of the crop of social entrepreneurs, scientists, university professors, inventors, and even astronauts presented on a variety of topics, including AI, nanobiology, space technology, machine learning, the future of medicine, and cyber threats. They also shared their observations on the most substantial bottlenecks humans were currently facing, but also where they thought technology could offer the most influential solutions. I was one of the few humanists selected that year. My ticket-winning idea was related to using virtual reality to help survivors of intimate partner violence find healing and take steps to rebuild their faith in life. The suffering of the hundreds of millions globally each year impacted by such violence is a tragedy, and it has a ripple effect—the resultant trauma also translates to wider long-term impacts in the workforce, health care, and our communities.

In the Global Solutions Program, I also realized that exponential technology alone might not be such a Holy Grail after all. While the promises are fairly evident, some applications of exponential technology may come with ambiguous or even outright harmful outcomes: controlling the human genome, for example, or helping small groups of elites consolidate power over the masses. At the end of those two months, I left Singularity University with a suitcase stuffed with notebooks full of ideas, plans, drawings, and diagrams about how to approach the bleak situation faced by humanity and how to hopefully use technology to solve them.

For all the tech and high-flying inventions that inspired me during the program, one major takeaway had been with me the entire time. I'd already suspected it in my research: our greatest potential as humans is the condition of our character. It's also our greatest detriment. This takeaway was beautifully highlighted by Kentaro Toyama during the program. Toyama is the W. K. Kellogg professor at the University of Michigan School of Information, an entrepreneur, computer scientist, and author of the bestselling book *Geek Heresy: Rescuing Social Change from the Cult of Technology*. His message to our classroom was direct and sobering: technology isn't a miracle drug; it simply amplifies whatever underlying forces are already present.

Six years later, when I had the chance to interview Toyama for this book, he was curious about the idea of gentle power. When I asked him about the future of humanity, he said that he was still optimistic about people in general, and he thought that our biggest opportunity and gift remains our immense capacity for growth. "Something inside of us wants that growth even though we don't consistently pursue it. That for me in the long term is the most promising aspect regarding what I think human beings might be able to do," he shared.[3]

Toyama's message reminded me that we all have power and potential within us; it's also on us to tap into them to bring forth something helpful and beautiful into the world. I also realized that technology is just like sisu. It simply amplifies what's already within us. Sisu and technology are both tools we can use in various ways, and the outcomes of that usage depend on the consciousness employing them. For example, we can use VR to help heal PTSD and support personal growth, or we can use it to perpetuate systems of violence, abuse, and oppression through pornography and violent gaming simulations. The types of seeds we plant matter, but so does the quality of the soil.

Cindy Mason is a research associate in the Stanford University computer science department who's working to design and program advanced AI computer systems that have the capacity for positive emotions, compassion, and human empowerment. One of these projects is intended to support people who experience loneliness. Mason also shared with me how AI can be trained to recognize facial expressions and other forms of nonverbal communication to glean human intent. She hopes that AI can help reduce the violence and abuse humans are capable of inflicting on each other by placing it in situations that will prevent harm—not just physically, but emotionally, socially, and financially. Mason believes that since AI is going to affect all of us in the future, it needs to be open to all members of society—including minorities, vulnerable populations, and those who have been silenced in the past or not listened to by those in power or favor. "Without equality, diversity, and justice, it is difficult to have the kind of caring and compassion that fuels cooperation. It is my hope that AI can support us with that," she told me.[4]

Technology done right and in the right hands can be a tremendous aid, but we can't just sprinkle AI over everything and hope that our problems will go away. As Toyama notes, the opposite is also possible. In *New Power: How Anyone Can Persuade, Mobilize, and Succeed in Our Chaotic, Connected Age*, Jeremy Heimans and Henry Timms also remind us that leadership is always an expression and extension of the person using it. Even more equitable forms of power can be used for harmful purposes in the wrong hands.[5] For this reason, we are all better served by leaders who are trained, encouraged, and expected to practice gentle power. As the Benjamin Franklin quote I mentioned at the end of the last chapter suggests, the earlier we can get started, the better. Fortunately, some mainstream educational institutions are beginning to teach skills outside of the typical STEM scope related to emotional intelligence, communication, and even intuition.

There's no reason that brilliant brains and gentle hearts can't work together. A recent study suggests that heart rate variation works with our cognitive abilities to enable wise reasoning about complex social issues.[6] As the robot Maria says in director Fritz Lang's 1927 expressionist film *Metropolis*, "There can be no understanding between the hand and the brain unless the heart acts as mediator."[7] To make wise decisions under pressure requires more than pure reason; it calls for us to connect to the full range of our intelligence, including intuition and other gifts typically associated with the heart.

What I concluded most from my time at Singularity University is that the quality of our human connection is far more crucial of a lever in global change than all the digital advancements together. Exponential technology will have a lot to offer us in the times ahead, but it all still ultimately begins with us. With gentle power, we are more likely to engage exponential technology with deeper clarity, focus, and goodwill.

PART V

Gentle Power in Daily Life

CHAPTER 12:

Sadhana (What Every Leader Needs)

It is the only thing we can do, Klaas, I see no alternative: each of us must turn inward and destroy in himself all that he thinks he ought to destroy in others. And remember that every atom of hate we add into this world makes it still more inhospitable.

—ETTY HILLESUM[1]

"Nothing, especially love, can be mastered without practice," Janur Yasa said, quoting the words of psychoanalyst Erich Fromm. My eyes traced the details of a wooden pillar in the beautiful training space in the dojo Janur had built. As we began another training session in aikido, Janur continued, "And practice involves discipline, concentration, patience, and supreme concern." He finished the quote and raised his inquisitive eyes to gaze at us students. "Now, ask yourself, why are you here?" His question lingered in the dojo and invited all of us to examine our core intentions.

Sadhana is a Sanskrit term I learned in India almost fifteen years ago. While sadhana's complete meaning eludes the scope of this book as it denotes a devoted inquiry into the very nature of existence in pursuit of spiritual awakening, the word is sometimes simplified in English to refer to a daily practice. Sadhana has such significance to me that I have the word carved in my *bokken*, the wooden training sword we use in aikido. Gentle power isn't just a quality or capacity; it's a habit—a sadhana. In all likelihood, everyone you admire didn't get to where they are in life by accident; they kept at it day after day, developed beneficial habits, and persisted despite countless disappointments.

Accordingly, this part of the book highlights the importance of focused practice to bring your ideas and intentions into reality. This is where I invite you to develop your own sadhana and start integrating gentle power into your life in tangible, effective ways. Among other things, this means creating positive habits, emphasizing self-care and self-understanding, and applying the wisdom of systems intelligence.

The Power of Deliberate Practice

> It is evident that our organism has stored-up reserves of energy that are ordinarily not called upon . . . most of us continue living unnecessarily near our surface.

-WILLIAM JAMES[2]

I've kept the above quote nearby for over a decade. It reminds me to always stay curious and hopeful regarding my capacities, to consciously choose to rise above the surface in this endless, unfolding journey. Although mastering anything takes time, the famous Chinese proverb reminds us that the adventure begins with one step. Similarly, Robert Nadeau Shihan—the founder and head instructor of City Aikido in San Francisco, as well as one of O'Sensei's direct students—often reminds his students to "start with what is," meaning to attend fully to the present moment without getting stuck in whatever thoughts and feelings show up. The key is to practice being nonjudgmental and open.

Even so, forming new habits takes work. In a widely cited study, Philippa Lally and her research team examined the habits of ninety-six people over a twelve-week period. On average, it took about 66 days for a new habit to form, although it varied widely—anywhere between 18 and 254 days, in fact—depending on the behavior to be modified, the person, and their circumstances.[3] To make matters even more interesting, habit formation is also asymmetrical—our learning curve is typically quite steep before it plateaus out.

John Hayes, a cognitive psychology professor emeritus at Carnegie Mellon University, has been investigating the role of effort, practice, and knowledge in top performers for decades. Hayes has studied some of the most talented creators and experts in history—people such as Mozart and Picasso, for example—to understand how long it takes to become a master of a chosen craft. His research highlights at least two useful points. First, none of the people Hayes analyzed produced top-quality work without putting in about a decade of practice first. Hayes referred to this period (which was usually marked with little recognition) as the "ten years of silence."[4] This finding also aligns with Anders Ericsson's (much debated) theory suggesting that one needs to put in about ten thousand hours to become an expert at something.[5]

Imagine taking such a focused approach to developing something like gentle power, your ability to create psychological safety, or learning how to relax your nervous system through breathwork and visualization. In essence, that's exactly what some pro athletes and neurosurgeons do to access the calm focus they need to perform at such a high level. Skills like these are available to anyone willing to commit themselves to deliberate or purposeful practice. Optimal performance requires the ability to relate to stressful events in an entirely different way. What psychology calls *eustress*, for example, refers to high performance and feelings of excitement and motivation when encountering a certain level of stress. While distress can cause confusion, impaired decision-making, and even lead to burnout, eustress promotes focused attention, emotional balance, and rational thought.[8]

Growth and learning necessarily involve setbacks.

When we first learn something new, we can feel somewhat like elephants in a crystal shop, but over time our actions become smooth and less self-conscious. It's like that with gentle power too. The more we practice, the more natural it becomes. By viewing every experience we meet as an opportunity to learn, gentle power becomes increasingly ingrained in our thoughts and actions. Our brain is extraordinarily sensitive to experience, and the interactions it has with the environment alter its morphology in measurable ways.[9] *Neuroplasticity* refers to the capacity of the nervous system to change its structure and function over a lifetime, and whenever neural networks change, behavior (including mental behavior) changes as well. Psychologist Rick Hanson, who is well-known for his research on the neuroscience of happiness, has dedicated his research to understanding this very process. Hanson describes how our perceptions, thoughts, and feelings depend on the ever-changing nature of nearly one hundred billion neurons in conversation with each other (with nearly half a quadrillion connections between them). "Day after day, your mind is building your brain," he writes.[10]

Extensive studies on the brains of animals exposed to complex or enriched environments have shown development of superior higher-order cognitive abilities, which has led to an understanding of the significance of direct experience to brain changes and, therefore, behavior change and learning.[11] Pretty much every experience has the potential to alter the brain, at least briefly. While still lacking a solid body of empirical studies, *self-directed neuroplasticity* (SDN) through focused attention to direct one's actions (and thereby rewiring one's brain) is gaining traction as a treatment for obsessive-compulsive disorder.[12]

Even so, growth and learning necessarily involve setbacks. For that reason, patience, kindness, and clear evaluation free of harsh judgment are absolutely essential. When we review our experiences without the overlay of judgment, we allow our brain to perform its analytical function more efficiently. It's crucial to remember this when establishing our sadhana. It's also important to remind ourselves that while our nervous system can learn almost anything, it can't learn *everything*—especially all at once. In this game, less is often more.

Choose Your Practice with Care

In a world where nearly everything—music, TV shows, dinner, toothbrushes, data storage plans, and so on—has become awash in a jungle of unlimited options, it's important to remember that having more choices isn't always the best thing for us. This truth was highlighted for me a while back when I visited a health store to buy some protein powder. I asked the clerk to point me to the right aisle in the sea of tubes, boxes, and jars—all packaged with magical ingredients to enhance brain health, muscle repair, immunity, energy levels, and you name it. When I arrived at the appropriate spot, I was met with far more protein options than I knew what to do with. Being a researcher, I began analyzing my choices—ingredients, prices, bag sizes, and flavors (although it's almost impossible to tell from the outside what "green superwoman mix" is supposed to taste like). After spending longer than you'd think coming up with my leading choice (Phyto Fire Honeycomb Protein, for the record), I approached the register, ready to pay. At the last second, the clerk asked if I might prefer to change my selection to one that came with a free mixing bottle and towel. "No, thank you!" I managed to wheeze, and I exited the store, somehow dissatisfied and depleted.

Research actually suggests that people feel more empowered when faced with limited choices. The *paradox of choice* was originally researched by Sheena Iyengar and became popularized through Barry Schwartz's eponymous book on the subject. I remember Schwartz lecturing about his work when I was attending the positive psychology program. He explained that our dissatisfaction when faced with too many choices occurs because we unconsciously create an ideal and entirely illusory option from the best parts of the alternatives before us. Then we use that fabricated option to judge the available ones before us. The price we pay in the end for all of this doesn't simply involve money—it costs us time and emotional health as well. There are countless ways that the paradox of choice plays out in our daily lives, including in the world of dating. I've known people who have been single for a long time, for example, who long to find a partner, yet spend years rejecting even some pretty reasonable candidates because they're not quite the *perfect* version of the imaginary person they've created in their head.

This book, too, includes a lot of helpful ideas to manifest gentle power in your life. As you explore some of the approaches I've found useful on my personal journey, I invite you to lightly consider what might work for you and what makes you feel most excited. Approach your sadhana with a "less is more" standpoint and resist the urge to try to do everything. Instead, slow down and use your intuition to choose a practice or two to feel your way into gentle power and greater self-understanding. If you only focus on one thing that truly feels beneficial to you and do that one thing with care and consistency until you have integrated the habit, it's a big win—and it will change your life. You get to choose what that thing of your sadhana is, of course—meditation, better sleep, Authentic

Relating, or whatever else speaks to you outside this book. One wisely chosen area of change or a particular practice that we stick to—no matter how simple it may sound—can open an entire world of personal transformation for us. My mantras for myself are: "keep it simple" and "practice before perfection."

CHAPTER 13:

Systems Intelligent Leadership

Gentleness invents an expanded present.

–ANNE DUFOURMANTELLE[1]

A ccording to some of the leading environmental scientists of our time, we may have already arrived at the final chapter of human life. How long that chapter is (and if it has a sequel) depends on us. "Time is like gas; it fills the space it is given," said James Pawelski, my former teacher, when giving us an assignment that came with a tight deadline. There's an air of urgency as we come to grips with the idea that we might be running out of time on this planet.

As the late quantum physicist David Bohm said, what's needed most right now is "a new way of thinking."[2] I'll add that this new way of thinking requires us to leave behind our powerlessness, harshness, and sense of playing small. After all this time, we must finally learn to think for ourselves and act with others and the fate of the world in mind. Just as crabs need to break free of their shells and snakes need to shed their skins, we too must leave behind the outdated ideas and patterns that don't serve us.

The decisions we make now as parents, creators, citizens, leaders, and consumers will ultimately determine the legacy of humankind. I believe, as E. O. Wilson did, that our legacy can still be "a permanent paradise for human beings, or the strong beginning of one" built through "an ethic of simple decency to one another."[3] From watching myself and others thrive after overcoming trauma and open to more love, I'm convinced that we humans have what it takes to make that paradise happen. We'll need gentle power to get us there, and we'll also need *systems intelligence.*

The Third Master Key

I first heard about systems intelligence from the Finnish entrepreneur Nelli Såger in New York in 2012. It was one of those "flashbulb memory" moments in life that I'll never forget. It was early midday in midtown Manhattan, and the sun sparkled nonchalantly through the window when something in my heart shifted. I became so excited by what Nelli was talking about that I couldn't later stop researching systems intelligence and its founders, professors Raimo Hämäläinen and Esa Saarinen from Aalto University in Finland. Reading about it made every nerve in my body tingle.

Systems intelligence focuses on the betterment of human life. Whereas systems thinking is about understanding broad systems in order to improve them from the outside, systems intelligence approaches everything from the inside. This difference, I think, parallels the distinction between information and understanding. Information allows us to describe something; knowledge is how we apply that information. When knowledge is applied through love, it becomes wisdom. Add sisu as our inner reserve of strength and you have a foundation for gentle power.

As for the betterment of human life, Hämäläinen and Saarinen's work specifically looks into actions within a given system that generate exponentially greater effects in other aspects of that system. Some of these actions are what Karen Golden-Biddle calls *micro-moves*—seemingly minor behaviors that can come across as barely noticeable yet still communicate respect and encourage people to build momentum for change.[4] Examples of micro-moves include installing access ramps on store fronts, offering space during the workday for team members to share what they've learned and celebrate breakthroughs, and simply giving someone credit for doing a good job. When leaders take actions like these, it creates an environment that empowers people to reach beyond their assumed capacities to create desired change and generates what researchers Martha Feldman and Anne Khademian call *cascading vitality*.[5]

All of us live within complex networks of relationships and events that we contribute to in unique ways. All human life is fundamentally systemic, and our emotional states manifest in the broader context of systemic resonance. In any given network, negative and positive emotions (whether displayed publicly or tacitly experienced) have effects well beyond those experienced by the individual.[6] Becoming more aware of systems intelligence has been revolutionary in my own life and key for becoming increasingly attuned to the bigger picture and my role within the systems I belong to. Our mere presence, words, and actions can open doors for others, but they can just as easily close them. Through the frame of the nervous system, these doors open and close based on which part of us gets activated—namely, the relaxed parasympathetic system or the hyperalert sympathetic system designed to ensure survival.

We all know people who activate either of these in us. There are people with whom we feel at ease and expansive, and there are those with whom we seem to always be a bit on edge. These can be people we know well or those we consider strangers. But the question that systems intelligence gently invites us to reflect on is this: *How do other people feel around me?* This inquiry also has the potential to awaken us to what's possible in each moment. For example, when a certain person rubs you the wrong way, you don't always have to shrink from them and treat them as overwhelming. You could also think, *It appears she's had a tough day. I'm going to do my best to remain patient and see what I can learn*, or *I notice that this experience activates some strong emotions in me*, and simply observe the moment without judging it. This type of pattern disruption is systems intelligence in action.

You can't change your blueprint unless you can see it.

Adopting a systems intelligent approach to life goes hand in hand with our practices of discernment, reflection, and attunement to others. Over time, we more naturally gravitate toward anything that reflects gentle power—in ourselves, in others, and in the world. Imagine a world built on this approach, where—by default—we habitually influence each other in positive ways and open even more doors to unexpressed potentiality.

According to Hämäläinen and Saarinen, systems intelligence is also a form of human behavioral intelligence that each of us possesses, and we can use that intelligence to navigate complex and sometimes demanding interactions by engaging in self-inquiry on a daily basis.[7] As they state in

Being Better Better (cowritten with American systems theorist and educator Rachel Jones), the key to creating change lies in our ability to *think about our thinking* and reflect on the mental models we have, understanding that they act as the underlying blueprint to all of our actions. You can't change your blueprint unless you can see it, and modifying your blueprint changes the outcomes it produces.

Thinking About Thinking

As demonstrated by Dweck and her research team at Stanford University, our beliefs greatly determine our future behaviors. Mental models, especially those pertaining to our beliefs, are of central importance to systems intelligence because they offer us the biggest opportunity for change. In systems intelligence, we access more of these windows of opportunity by improving the quality of our thinking. For Hämäläinen and Saarinen, this includes:

- Acknowledging that our actions and behaviors are partially the result of our thinking (mental models, beliefs, assumptions, interpretations, etc.).

- Remembering that our thinking is likely one-sided and a far cry from an accurate grasp of the bigger picture. The holistic systems that surround us aren't always taken into consideration, or they're only done so in distorted ways.

- Acting more intelligently in the systemic environment by engaging in meta-level thinking regarding our own thinking.

- Seeing that our framing of the environment and its interconnected systems is likely just an image we carry built on subjective assumptions.[8]

Systems intelligence is like getting a new update for your inner software. We already have the right operating system; it's just that many of us haven't been taught to use it to its full potential. When I became more aware of the broad-reaching effects of my words and actions and realized that I could use my thinking to benefit myself and others, I started viewing everything and everyone I experienced with more curiosity and openness and way less judgment. Systems intelligence isn't just about thinking about thinking; it also asks us to bring greater attention to our behaviors and connections with others.

Micro-Moments

John Gottman and his colleagues at the University of Washington have studied what they call the *mathematics of marriage* and observed that one of the most significant challenges married couples face is the *regulating negative affect*. "The balance between negative and positive affect is absolutely critical in predicting the longitudinal fate of marriage," they assert.[9] By simply observing couples during conflict, the research team was able to reliably predict which couples would end up divorced, stable but unhappy, or stable and happy within the next six years of their lives. Happy-stable couples enjoyed thirty more seconds of positive affect (affection, humor, and engaged listening, for example) out of nine hundred seconds observed than unhappy-stable couples. In turn, those unhappy-stable couples had thirty seconds more positive affect than the couples who eventually divorced.

Systems intelligence emphasizes the importance of choice in our day-to-day lives. The challenge is for us to recognize certain moments for their power and potential. You could say that some of the couples in Gottman's study could have chosen to listen or smile more, offer a comforting embrace, or reply with a kind word instead of sarcasm for example. We regularly dismiss the relevance of positive micro-behaviors like these, instead defaulting to indifference, mediocrity, or habitual negativity. Few people would say that they want a mediocre relationship, and yet without much sense of agency they turn a blind eye to patterns—in themselves and their partner—that create mediocrity.

Here's an idea: the next time you're with someone close to you (a partner or friend, for example), in your mind make a conscious note of their positive qualities. Look for what is wonderful about them—and consider sharing it with them too. Try this practice our for some days or a week and then give it a shot on someone you don't know as well—the bus driver, the cashier at the grocery store, or people at work. Remember that our brains are hardwired to notice what's negative or harmful in our environment, but this leaves out a substantial portion of the picture. This is the part where we get to choose what we focus on. "There is more to us than meets the eye," as professor Esa Saarinen likes to say.

Rick Hanson compares the mind to a garden. We can all think of ourselves as gardeners—we foster the flowers and remove the weeds. Hanson describes three ways to do to this: *let be, let go,* or *let in.* We can nurture what's good by looking at the flowers and weeds (that is, the good and the bad) without judgment and by pruning and watering accordingly.[10] Some of us—myself included at times—don't often consider that we have a choice in the matter, simply because we're overly stressed or concerned with just getting by. But when I choose to pay more attention to what's good in my life, I notice how considerately my partner handed me the keys to our home, I really take in the way that the clerk at the grocery store looked at me straight in the eyes with full presence as she greeted me, and I gratefully recognize the effort my Balinese landlord put into sending a thoughtful text like: "It's nice to have you back home, even if for just one night." These are all examples of how people I've recently encountered chose to infuse the systems around them with beauty and gentleness.

Try to notice moments like these in your own life and respond accordingly. For the above examples, I could have said, "Thank you, sweetheart, for thinking of me and pulling out the right key so it's easier for me to open the door in the dark," and "You have an amazing smile, dear sister. Thank you for making my day," and "Thanks for being such a caring landlord and putting in effort to make me feel at home in a foreign country." Simple responses like these highlight the good and encourage others to continue to make positive micro-behaviors.

While focusing on small gestures like these might not seem like such a big deal, systems intelligence theorists encourage leaders to practice and model them because of the powerful positive impact of such conscious leadership practices on organizational cultures. And whether we think of ourselves as leaders or not, our lives are powerfully affected by straightforward gestures and comments like these that are almost always within our reach.

Systems of Holding Back

A world that's unsafe, unsustainable, and uncaring is a reality that nobody in their right mind wants. Most spouses would love to enjoy amazing emotional and physical intimacy with their partners, and most leaders would love to offer outstanding support for their teams. And yet—when we look around at the current state of the world—poverty, refugee crises, hunger, social disconnection, addiction, and abusive relationships are way more prominent that any of us would choose.

In a world of such abundance, why is this the case? One explanation is that patterns of scarcity easily develop when generosity is called for but is not practiced. These patterns lead people to hold back contributions, affirmations, and acknowledgment simply because they perceive (or believe they perceive) others holding back something they would experience as meaningful or benefitting. As Hämäläinen and Saarinen caution, "Human interaction has a tendency to slide into systems of holding back unless conscious effort is launched to counter this tendency."[11]

I attended an opening keynote speech by Peter Senge in Finland in 2014. The author of *The Fifth Discipline* was attending an event organized by the Systems Analysis Laboratory of Aalto University. Senge spoke on the poor environmental situation in Los Angeles where he grew up, where the demand for economic growth transformed the area from a virtual Eden into a concrete jungle. He explained how even as a young boy, he understood that no one purposefully wanted to destroy the orange groves, ruin the places children loved to play, or foul the air with pollution, and yet, that's exactly what happened.[12] Similarly, poor leadership, unethical business practices, or a lack of psychological safety in families aren't things that anyone intentionally sets out to create. No one wants pandemics and climate disruption. Even so, humans have destroyed a tenth of the planet's remaining wilderness in the last twenty-five years, pushing species out of their habitats and into extinction.[13] As Senge said in the lecture mentioned above, "It doesn't really help much to have systems awareness up here [in one's head]. It comes down to what we do, how we operate, how we think and act."

Unfortunately, even people who are inclined to action often have trouble knowing where to start. The systems intelligence approach begins by avoiding blame and fault-finding and working instead with the *nonlife-generating systems* in order to find openings for growth and change. Hämäläinen and Saarinen suggest that instigating micro-behaviors of encouragement, support, and respect is always a good place to start because these actions—along with excitement, energy, and elevation—are fundamental to the human condition. Accordingly, these are all places where leaders are encouraged to focus their efforts.[14]

> ## Whoever you are and whatever your concerns happen to be, there's something positive you can do in this very moment.

While our developmental history, attachment styles, inherited beliefs, and cultural expectations have a lot of say in how we act, we regularly have more choice than we might recognize. While we all suffer from unhealthy systems, we also have the power to create something better— and it starts with our thinking. Being a gentle power leader in your family and professional life means to consciously promote growth and the betterment of life for all concerned. It's about always being on the lookout for what's good in each other and what's positive in each moment and, in doing so, encouraging all of that to blossom. If your relationship could use more intimacy, that means taking the first step—light some candles around the house, offer your beloved a massage, or simply allow them to vent for a moment about their day without judgment or unrequested advice. If you're a leader who wants to create an environment of support, that means taking the time to be present with your employees, building a sense of community, and consciously looking for ways to encourage them. And if you're someone who's concerned about the environment, it means directing your money to environmentally conscious companies, planting trees, or cultivating a love for nature in your children. Whoever you are and whatever your concerns happen to be, there's something positive you can do in this very moment.

I Can Choose

My ability to sense, embrace, adjust, and navigate my inner and outer environments is what determines my growth and expression as a gentle power leader. I believe that systems intelligence, when practiced deliberately, can offer a path to creating conditions not only conducive to sisu, but to sisu that is healthy and balanced for individuals and the systems in which they live.

My aikido teacher Janur once said, "It's easy to be clever. It's much harder to be loving." I've found that to be true time and time again. But even the times when I struggle to remain soft and compassionate or when I fail to stand up and express my truth are opportunities for growth and strength. Even when my gentle power wavers, just paying attention to that fact is helpful. Hope is inherent to all life and all systems, and they, in turn, continually evolve. Developing systems intelligence requires trying things out and testing ideas. In doing so, we acknowledge both our incompleteness and vast wonderfulness.

For some of us, self-kindness is a lot harder to perform than kindness toward others. It's important that we recognize our shortcomings without flogging ourselves for them. We don't want to act things out unconsciously, but we also must keep in mind the *gentle* polarity of gentle power. The most impressive things we do aren't typically the sort of accolades we can put on a CV; usually they're about choosing forgiveness over being right, prioritizing presence over profit, gravitating toward growth rather than pride, and attuning to the best course of action regardless of what the what the general masses might say. Sometimes we need self-forgiveness when the gravity of missed opportunities begins to drag us down. We can activate our gentle power in these moments simply by offering ourselves a kind, forgiving hand.

The new era of enlightenment is calling us to wake up to our ability to think and reason with clarity but also to our ability to feel, intuit, and navigate by heart. In this way, we can heal those parts of us that have been stiffened by the plight of survival—our own and the world's. We start to feel ourselves and each other again. This is where reason and emotion are invited to the same table, and the outcome of their union is gentle power. It's the next step of our evolution as a species.

For the next week or so, observe yourself in your particular systems (these include anything from your intimate and casual relationships to your workplace and the communities you are part of, and even the environment around you) and notice any potential opportunities to enact positive micro-behaviors. You can also look for patterns of withholding. Record your observations (including your emotions and how others react to you) in a journal or notebook. Write down at least five moments from each day and reflect on the experience at the end of the week.

CHAPTER 14:

The Alchemy
of Gentle Power

*Out of clutter, find simplicity. From discord, find
harmony. In the middle of difficulty lies opportunity.*

—ALBERT EINSTEIN[1]

Alchemy is the ancient practice of transforming a common substance into one of substantially greater value. In Paulo Coelho's *The Alchemist*, this transformation is from lead into gold, which is an excellent metaphor for turning our everyday experiences into gemlike wisdom and understanding. In turn, this understanding brings us more alignment, clarity, and empowered peace of mind. In this final chapter, I want to offer some key discoveries to help you unlock your own understanding and view your own life as a series of opportunities to transmute lead into gold. Every challenge and misstep can lead to more learning; every victory can remind us of our resourcefulness, courage, and strength. Everything is a potential lesson in the dojo of life.

Earlier I mentioned how Janur Yasa asked his aikido students, "Why are you here?" I invite you now to ask the same question. Slow down and gently ask, "Why did I choose to read this book? What do I want to get out of it?" Think about that for a few minutes, write down your responses, and then ask yourself, "What am I searching for? What do I want to create in my life right now?" Your answers to these questions will help you put together a personal sadhana to enhance your leadership and cultivate gentle power.

Succeed with Grace

One of the most profound moments of self-understanding I had during the fifty days in New Zealand happened in the morning of day eighteen. I'd been reading *Dancing in Her Own Moonlight*, a book written by Janelle Fletcher. She had stuffed a copy of it into my bag as I was leaving Wanaka a week and a half earlier and said, "Maybe you'll find some gems in here for your quest." I picked the book up a few days later and contemplated the reflective questions she'd sprinkled throughout. One question in particular stood out to me—it asked me to define what success means. *It means to lift others up and help them see their potential,* I thought. *Success also means growing in self-understanding and translating my gifts into positive actions.* Janelle's follow-up question was, "What does it look like to succeed with grace?" I thought a lot about this as I hit the next 50 km stretch that morning. What does it feel like to run, speak, and engage with grace? The answers eluded me at first, just as sisu once did. But eventually it occurred to me that grace is refined and embodied, just as gentle power is. It's not just that we're *being* gentle; we have *become* gentleness.

Think about the dynamic yet effortless movement of a ballerina or how swans glide elegantly upon the surface of a lake. Grace isn't forced; it simply *is*. Even so, there's a lot more going on than meets the eye. In the case of the ballerina, what appears so effortless comes from years of repeating certain movements. The ballerina has practiced her sadhana to allow the masterpiece of grace to become inseparable from her physical form. In the case of the relaxed and regal swans, what we view on the surface is generated by the vigorous and invisible movement of their feet paddling beneath the water. Grace is an embodied reality of unforced and unrushed power, and it's available to every one of us.

For a moment, entertain the idea that grace is your core essence. Grace is you in your natural state. Grace is what lies beneath the disturbing waves of the overly active ego as it tries to control, please, avoid, and placate in the name of safety. It doesn't matter who you are or how distracted, disturbed, or unbalanced you might feel; grace is a potential of less contraction and more calmness available to you in every moment.

On the morning I referred to above, as I contemplated what it meant to run gracefully, I started noticing how my posture became more upright, yet soft. I also noticed that my pace slowed down and that I was more aware of my surroundings. From the perspective of function and performance, I was doing exactly the same thing I'd been doing for weeks—moving my body forward using my legs and feet—but on that day, the miles rolled by differently. It reminded me of a line from the *Tao Te Ching*: "Nature doesn't hurry and yet everything gets done."[2]

The alchemy of everyday magic is always right there in front of us. It's when a friend asks to meet for coffee, but we really need to work or rest, or when the boss asks for overtime when we've already made a family commitment, or when our romantic partner asks us what's wrong and we have a hard time replying honestly. All these situations are opportunities to unlearn habits of yielding instinctively or not speaking our truth, as well as opportunities to leave behind any patterns that sway us from our center and to finally embody the grace that returns us there across the bridge of truth. More often than we think, we're given just the right moment to practice honesty with ourselves and others, set healthy boundaries, and choose vulnerability in the name of true intimacy.

I've included some contemplative questions in this chapter to support your journey. I warmly encourage you to use your special notebook if you have one to answer these questions, so you can keep a track of your gentle power journey. Below each of them, you'll find an affirmation to anchor the message in daily practice, and I encourage you to let those messages sink in by taking a moment to reflect and writing down any thoughts that come to you. You can read the affirmations out loud or in silence, but whatever you do, truly feel into what arises for you. If something helpful comes up, be sure to make a note of it (I like using a moderate amount of sticky notes.) and place that note where you'll see it often. Here's the first set of questions, modified from those asked by my friend Janelle:

Questions to Contemplate

- What does success look like for you?
- In your daily life, what would it look like to succeed with grace?

Affirmation for Learning Gentle Power with Ease

I trust the process of life to open me to the wisdom of my leardership in a way that is engaged but unhurried, committed but uncontracted. I am not here to achieve anything but simply to remember my natural capacity for strength and love. Rather than striving or seeking to fix myself or others, I am here to cultivate the spirit of nonjudgment and unwinding. When I let go of any fierceness created by force, I make space for the grace that illuminates my everyday experience with ease.

> There's usually more love, patience,
> compassion, understanding, and graceful
> strength available to us than we think.

Grace Under Pressure

Dean Karnazes is an American ultrarunner who some years ago completed the grueling *Spartathlon*—a 153-mile race of thirty-four hours of nonstop running from Athens to Sparta in Greece. Dean later told me during an interview that he was, needless to say, completely spent. The only thing on his mind was heading straight to his accommodation so he could begin the process of recovery. However, as he crossed the finish line, Dean saw that there was a crowd of people who'd waited a long time to greet him. "There were moments when I thought I might blackout," Dean told me. "I'd just completed this insanely difficult ultramarathon and been running for nearly a day and a half without sleep." Even though they couldn't possibly relate to how exhausted he was, Dean chose to stay with them before heading to his hotel. "I found the extra reserve of inner strength to spend a couple hours with the people talking, signing books, taking photos, and just giving myself over to something bigger than me," he said.[3]

Dean's example is a wonderful story of how it's possible to exemplify immense amounts of sisu and still remain caring and present. At the end of that seemingly impossible run, what shone through most was Dean's human capacity for warmth—in other words, sisu in its highest expression: gentle power. It's not too difficult to be loving and graceful when we're full of energy and well-rested and when everything has gone according to the plan. However, bring in the crazy energy of a busy Monday morning, rush-hour traffic, the wonky full moon, and so on, and something dreadful happens even to the best of us. It's entirely human, and the point here isn't to expect the impossible from ourselves or push ourselves past our very reasonable limits. The point is that there's usually more love, patience, compassion, understanding, and graceful strength available to us than we think. And with practice and preparation, we can access all of that and more.

"Leadership is a personal ethos," Dean told me. "A leader holds to their values and a higher standard regardless of the situation or temptation." The ability to do so takes work. Whether we hold ourselves to the standard of patience and gentleness when our children are screaming at us or whether it's giving time to supporters after running for days on end, exhibiting grace under pressure matters when it's called for, and we can all prepare for those moments for when they inevitably arise. When he is on the road, Damian Hall—another ultra-distance runner—helps prep himself for such time with a "swift daily sob."[4] Whatever it looks like, our sadhana is what gets us ready for whatever challenges and surprises the journey has in store for us.

I thought about Dean's story a lot when I was running in New Zealand. It set a precedent for how I wanted to carry myself when depleted because I was constantly meeting people for the Sisu Not Silence campaign when I was utterly exhausted. Thinking of how Dean stayed present for the people who came to greet him and shower him with appreciation inspired me to find that extra something inside when it mattered. For example, when I ran from Queenstown to Wanaka across the Crown Range on day six, I arrived at Wanaka much later than expected and had very little time to shower, recover, and prepare myself to speak at one of our events. I sat in silence for a few moments before I went on to present. My feet and head ached, but my heart was steady and strong. I opened my eyes, walked out to personally welcome nearly eighty guests, delivered my speech, and hugged people on their way out while gifting them a sisu wristband. I was showered with love, curiosity, and warmth, and I wouldn't have traded that experience for the world.

Questions to Contemplate

- When have I witnessed grace under pressure? What did it look like, and how did it make me feel?
- When is it good or necessary to go the extra mile for others? When is it not okay? How can I know the difference?

Affirmation for Grace Under Pressure

There is great wisdom unfolding in me that relates to the simple beauty of slowing down and choosing presence over performance and progress over perfection. Each moment offers me an opportunity to gently hold both my grounded and unmovable strength and the sweetness of everyday empathy. I embrace my potential while also accepting my humanness. When I need to retract from service to rest, I can do so with firm gentleness.

Be the One

I once read a story in *Helsingin Sanomat* (the leading Finnish newspaper) with an unusual headline: "Former Patient of a Lockdown Ward Set to Defend Her Doctoral Dissertation." I was so moved by the story that I reached out to the woman in question by email and asked if I could meet her. Thankfully, Päivi Rissanen agreed.

After earning her master's in social work and working for a while, Päivi told me that she fell into psychotic depression with repeating patterns of self-harm. She was admitted to a psychiatric hospital, where a few weeks turned into several years, and Päivi eventually found herself on a lockdown ward where she had been labeled as a hopeless case that the nurses were outright reluctant to work with. It was hard for me to correlate that story with the image of the articulate woman in front of me, sipping coffee in her black winter coat. Listening to Päivi, I was reminded once again of the immense fortitude of the human spirit, as well as the power outsiders sometimes have in our lives.

Päivi's *deus ex machina* arrived in the form of Juha, a semi-reluctant and stern nurse who had been assigned to her case. One day he asked Päivi point-blank, "So Päivi, tell me really. Is your plan to stay here for the rest of your life?" Neither of them knew it then, but this question was the first of many that became the catalyst for lasting change. Juha and Päivi created an instruction manual for *Super Päivi*—the woman she was on a good day, the woman who wasn't repeatedly trying to harm herself. The manual offered her meaningful and guiding questions for homework, and after only two months, Päivi was discharged to an open ward. Fourteen years later, against all odds—and partially against the advice of concerned university staff who were worried about her ability to follow through with such a major endeavor—Päivi defended her doctoral thesis at the University of Helsinki on the topic of mental illness and rehabilitation that was based on her own experience and recovery.[5]

Päivi told me that what changed the game for her was Juha's courage to challenge her and his ability to see her as a human first—that is, not as a hopeless psychiatric case. Her work and inner heavy lifting to follow through with years of healing, recovery, and rebuilding are all a testimony to Päivi's inner fortitude and sisu, but also to the role that Juha played, which speaks to the efficacy of gentle power leadership to help others engage their full potential. This is why I called this section *"Be the One."* As leaders, we can't wait for others to step in. As the saying goes, *We're the ones we've been waiting for.*

Every day, life gives us opportunities to open a door for someone in much the same way. We often can't know the full power of a smile, caring words, or even an honest reflection that models self-understanding and self-acceptance. When we choose to *be the one*, we choose to be on the lookout for facilitating moments wherein our presence can empower, generate trust and safety, and guide others into their own gentle power. Just as some seeds can remain buried for years but have innate coding that under the right conditions (temperature, water, nutrition) activates them to sprout and reach toward sunlight, the creativity, sisu, and gentle power of every one of us is always looking for an opportunity to grow. As Päivi's story illustrates, when we receive the ingredients we most need, we naturally self-repair and evolve. In other words, magic happens.

One of my classmates from the University of Pennsylvania positive psychology program was Robert Easton, the now retired senior managing director of Accenture in Australia and New Zealand. Bob is working on a PhD on *trust* and he once told me that the brilliance of an organization ultimately comes down to the smallest moments of connection between individuals that he calls "the in-betweens." I think we too often fail to create the lives we want simply because we forget the power of these connections, as well as the ordinary magic of choosing to *be the one*. As Jane Dutton says, "Each one of us has a magic wand where, by how we interact with others, we can, with our relational wand, leave others better off."[6]

I once gave a speech to an audience of business execs and HR managers at a conference at Finlandia Hall in Helsinki. I began with an obvious statement: "We all want safety, happiness, and success." When we receive those things, it typically means that we're leading meaningful lives at work and at home. While there are pockets of this goodness everywhere, the statistics are sobering. For example, 83 percent of workers in the United States suffer from work-related stress, which is enough to result in $190 billion in health care costs yearly and 120,000 deaths.[7] If we all desire happiness so much, how does that statistic make sense? If we value safety, why do nearly 300 million children witness family violence every year?[8] Something isn't adding up. We know enough from philosophy, psychology, spirituality, and our own commonsense to determine what promotes the good life and what doesn't, so what's standing in the way?

The Finnish icon of architecture Alvar Aalto (who also designed the iconic Finlandia Hall where I was delivering the talk) once said: "Architecture must have charm; it is a factor of beauty in society. But real beauty is not a conception of form . . . it is the result of harmony between several intrinsic factors, not the least, the social."[9] That's the answer I keep returning to. Abundance and well-being don't come from our cleverness or willpower; they come from our human connections—from all that which happens *in-between* you and me. When I played treasure-hunting games as a kid, the map to the prize was always marked with an *X*. In gentle power leadership, that *X* is what happens every day between me and every person I meet. It's the same with you too. That alchemical space between us and others is where the answers lie. It's a place available to us where we can turn all of this lead into gold.

As leaders, sometimes we need to be soft and pliable, and sometimes we must be firm and unshakeable. The art of gentle power asks us to learn how to harmonize these polar approaches in order to take the right action at the right moment to benefit everyone involved. Doing so is a lifelong path, but it's a path that is always right beneath our feet, especially when we choose to *be the one*.

Questions to Contemplate

- Has someone noticed your potential before you could recognize it yourself? How did their recognition influence how you view yourself? How did it change your life?

- Who do you know who might be an alchemist in disguise? Whose sisu and gentle power can you acknowledge right now in order to remind them of their own magic and potential?

Affirmation to Nurture the Insight of Gentle Power

As I patiently work on my insight, I remain on the lookout for opportunities to remind others of their potential and gifts. I do this with gentle power, which means I am honest but always loving. I am not here to change anyone but to simply offer a hand, shoulder, or ladder as needed. I trust the process, potential, and passion of others just as I trust mine. As I remain tenderly open to the power and beauty in others, I touch into my own graceful strength through the art of service.

Self-Care Means Taking Your Power Back

In a culture that glorifies busyness and applauds overachievement, overtime, and cutting play in pursuit of greater profit, self-care is often a dirty word to those who view prioritizing one's own well-being as idle, selfish, unfocused, or lazy. Here, it is a foundational quality of a gentle power leader. In this final section, I want to emphasize some direct forms of self-care that can work wonders—sleep, nutrition, relationships, and a daily practice for inner development. All of these will patch up energy leaks, ground you, help you prioritize life choices that fuel you, and connect you to healthy sisu—which, put simply, is life energy. When we take care of ourselves, we're better able to love others. For this reason, self-care is the foundation for gentle power.

Let's start with one of the biggies: sleep. Sleep is power. When we sleep, our cells regenerate, our brain rids itself of toxins, and our entire system resets to carry us through the next daily cycle. Insufficient sleep is commonly associated with impaired cognitive functioning, obesity, and a host of other physical and mental challenges. Recent studies suggest that poor sleep is such a global issue that it should be considered a health epidemic.[10]

Even so, most of us cut corners when it comes to our rest time. I used to brag about my ability to get by on only four to five hours of sleep a night. It was like a badge of honor; I thought of it as stealing daylight from the night or stealing from death itself (because, I reasoned, being awake meant more life). I couldn't have been more wrong. Have you ever heard a professional athlete brag about how *little* they slept the night before a big race or competition? Ultrarunners might be a little crazy, but most of them are well-known for their dedication to repairing their bodies and keeping track of their physical well-being constantly. More than skill, hard work, or talent, *recovery* and preservation of one's life energy are the keys to high performance, creativity, and our ability to navigate pressure with clarity, discernment, and grace.

All of us can enhance our self-care by making sure that we establish and maintain healthy routines. That starts with adequate sleep, nourishing movement (preferably in nature), and whatever diet works best for you. If these three aspects of self-care aren't already in place for you, take a week just to track them. Apps are great for recording this kind of data and making sense of it for you, but simply writing it all down in your notebook or journal works just fine. Note the times when you go to bed and when you wake up, the amount and quality of your sleep, and what you do immediately before bedtime. Track your exercise and recreational movement—the time spent, intensity, and so on—as well as the types of food, snacks, and fluids you consume over the course of the week (water, alcohol, caffeine, sugar, processed edibles, and natural foods). Most importantly, each morning and evening note your overall mood or level of life energy (you can, for example, evaluate it numerically, with 10 being top notch and 0 being the lowest possible). Write some notes too to describe what's going on. These will help you later to detect patterns and gain understanding of yourself.

The next step is to assess this data after a week. Does anything stand out to you? What do you feel best about? What would you like improve? Do you see any patterns between your mood and amount of sleep or other self-care activities? The main thing at this point is to gain awareness of your habits and start asking questions. I once tracked my bedtime habits on a piece of paper for a week: hours slept and a smiley or frowny face to indicate my mood that day. It was simple and sobering to notice the instant connection of the two variables. Along the way, you too will discover that it isn't so difficult to monitor your patterns and identify small tweaks that have large effects when it comes to your well-being. Systems intelligence (which I introduced in chapter 13) means to observe a system, get the feedback, and keep making incremental intelligent changes on the fly to improve how things work!

Self-care, just like gentle power, is a habit. Practice any habit long enough and it will stick. You don't need to enroll in an expensive self-improvement program, sign your life over to a fitness guru, or purchase the latest gadgets to make positive changes to your sleep, exercise, or diet, although prominent advertisements might say otherwise. There's also no need to *utterly* revolutionize your sleeping habits, go on a crazy diet, or pick some intense activity in order to feel more engaged and nourished. In fact, repeatedly taking up activities that are too extreme or intense can become a distraction from putting in the time-tested but sometimes tedious work of patiently building deep-seated habits that last when the novelty wears out. Many of us, including myself, have fallen back into old routines because it was too hard to maintain something new that started way too intense. Besides, most of us already know (at least, intuitively) what makes us feel more alive and stronger—and often these are in fact simple things. When we apply our minds to it, most of us also know what we're doing to leave ourselves stressed out and depleted. The simple tracking and analysis practice above is just a way of gently reminding yourself of what you already know and may be just the prompt you need to get back on your proverbial horse.

You might also feel that your self-care routines are solid or at least as healthy as you can pull off right now. That is great, but if that's not the case for you, just pick an area that calls to you and get started. You could commit to getting a minimum eight to nine hours of sleep each night for a week, for example, or limit your screen time before bedtime to enhance better sleep. One basic thing I did was to buy an old-fashioned alarm clock, so I have no real reason to keep my phone within reach. You could however set notifications on your phone in the daytime to remind you to drink more water, eat your favorite vegetable or fruit, or track your intermittent fasting, if that's your thing. Or you could make a promise to yourself to take three long walks (or jogs or sprints, depending on your current conditioning) over the course of the week and add a few minutes of stretching into each hour of sitting. Or do a few push-ups every time you get a refill of water, visit the bathroom, and so on. Then reflect on how it feels compared to sitting in front of your computer for long hours or being inactive for extended periods.

Whatever you choose, keep it simple, especially when you're just beginning. That's the key for follow-through. While there might be a temptation to cut corners to make up for any previous bad habits, too much too soon is not a winning recipe for lasting change—and it's especially contradictory to developing habits of gentle power. If you want to try to change too much all at once, remember that overly ambitious New Year's resolutions aren't known to work for very long. Just pick one that seems most important right now—sleep, exercise, or diet. Try it out for a week or so and be sure to track any positive changes to your mood, energy level, mental clarity, ability to solve problems, creativity, and so on.

Relationships are also crucial to self-care. I encourage my clients to pay attention to who they spend the most time with and honestly reflect on how these relationships make them feel. As with sleep, movement, and nutrition, the general rule of thumb is to do more of what makes you energized and empowered. Sometimes we find ourselves in turbulent relationships, but we excuse the rough weather because these people feel crucial to our ongoing growth. In fact, we might be thankful for how they reveal our triggers and engage those parts of us that need more attention or work. That can be tricky, of course. We all need the fire of transformation in our lives, but too much of it can leave us burned or burned-out.

Relationships aren't as easy to track as sleep or glasses of water, and there's no one-size-fits-all solution that I've ever encountered. Just do your best to make sure those closest to you are encouraging both the gentle side in you as well your expression of your healthy power. And of course, make sure that you in turn are doing the same.

There's a lot more that I learned about myself and self-care during my time in New Zealand. For example, how much in the past I gravitated toward adversity and turbulence. Reviewing my life, I saw that it regularly took tremendous challenge and pain for me to grow or learn something important, almost as if I required regular exposure to fire-breathing dragons in order to thrive. Whether it was facing my trauma and fear, working through a conflict with a friend or partner, or addressing some larger disturbance in the world, I had a habit of walking right up to the dragon, sticking my head in its mouth, and digging around in there for whatever treasure of transformation I could find. It's fine to be brave, but when bravery becomes a thing in itself—instead of being a vehicle for gaining understanding and growth—we can get stuck in a rut of reexperiencing pain more than is necessary.

There's nothing wrong with this approach. Some of us just need dragons in our life, at least for a little while. But over time, I realized they weren't as helpful to me as they once had been, and I put my head into more than one futile dragon mouth despite my better judgment. What also made a world of difference, thanks to Diane Poole Heller (mentioned in chapter 5), was to finally understand my attachment style. Seeing all this helped me switch the pattern. Instead of struggle, I decided to give alignment and ease a go, if only as an experiment. For now, that's what works better for me, and it influences everything I do these days—the types of work projects I take on, how much traveling I do, and the relationships I choose to put the most time and heart into—how I lead myself. It doesn't mean I shy away from big dreams and goals. It simply means that the energy with which I approach any endeavor has changed. Remember the wisdom I quoted earlier from the *Tao Te Ching*: "Nature doesn't hurry and yet everything gets done." Changing your overall approach to life toward more ease can be self-care too—and it can result in unrivaled benefits.

You're in charge of your life. While we all have varying amounts of access to things that contribute to our freedom to choose, we almost always have a say on who we spend time with and how we choose to learn. If nothing else, this includes choosing which thoughts drive our feelings, actions, and self-talk. To this end, it's important to pay attention to how you speak to yourself as well as any areas of laxity or overthought. For example, some of us have a habit of overthinking things to the detriment of our sleep and general mental well-being. Some of us have a habit of preferring chaos to stability. And some of us—especially in our work—have a habit of playing small in order to stay safe. Self-care means looking into all of this too.

Finally, a related pillar of self-care is the time we make to nourish inner stillness, presence, and connection to something greater than ourselves (whether you call it the Divine, God, the universe, your Higher Self, or whatever name best works for you). It's crucial that our sadhana includes this often-overlooked aspect of life, whether that means prayer, scripture, meditation, time alone in the woods, or my favorite—silence—which is presence with no story. If nothing else, find room for silence in your life. In a world driven toward exponential connectivity and stimulation, silence is truly golden. Our nervous system is bombarded with digital data, meaning that those brilliant survival mechanisms that kept our species alive for thousands and thousands of generations are typically in overdrive. Just as a turtle pulls its head and feet inside its protective shell from time to time, we could also benefit from regular withdrawal into our inner caves of silence.

Self-care is self-power.

Regardless of one's spiritual inclinations, countless studies have shown meditation to be beneficial for sleep, focus, tranquility, and general well-being. Among them, Sara Lazar and her team at Harvard University found that meditation can increase cortical thickness in parts of the brain (for example, the hippocampus) that are connected to learning and memory.[11] One of the reasons mediation works is because it reduces activation of what's known as the default mode network (DMN) and returns the mind to the present moment. The DMN is associated with mental wandering and ruminating thoughts—what is known in some traditions (and experienced by many of us) as the *monkey mind*. Even if our awareness likes to jump from one thing to the next like a monkey, that type of frenetic

THE ALCHEMY OF GENTLE POWER

activity for too long can make us irritable, unfocused, and dissatisfied. Thankfully, meditation is an easily accessible tool to bring any of us back to stillness. You don't have to travel to a ten-day silent retreat in the mountains or chant 108 different names of Hindu goddesses unless it calls to you. Research shows that even a regular meditation practice of ten to twenty minutes a day can offer tremendous benefits.

Self-care is self-power. By attending to your well-being, you'll have way more physical and mental resources to function and face any curveballs the world throws your way. Life can get away from us sometimes, and self-care is a way to make sure we have more say-so in the matter. So do what you can to get enough quality sleep, exercise in rewarding and healthy ways, practice the eating habits that work best for your body, enjoy nourishing relationships, and connect to the deeper stillness and peace that is your birthright.

Questions to Contemplate

- What are my nonnegotiables for self-care? What do I need in terms of sleep, exercise, rest, nutrition, relationships, and my practices for inner growth?
- What shifts in my life when I truly prioritize well-being and harmony?
- Think about a situation in which you were asked to do something but felt conflicted about saying yes. What would happen if you put alignment and honesty over obligation and people-pleasing?

Affirmation to Nurture More Gentle Power Through Self-Care

I am a precious being whose well-being matters, and I trust in my power to care for myself. I am not here to achieve anything but to experience life as fully as I can. I will stop glorifying busyness and make space for slowing down so I can live from a place of ease and harmony. I protect my nonnegotiables of self-care and have firm boundaries that I communicate with strength and kindness. I have full permission to care for myself, and pain is no longer the price I accept to pay for success.

Conclusion

I'm looking at the road ahead of me. It's curvy, long, and it
calls to me. I did not choose it; it chose me. I was brought
here through time, space, and experience to fulfill a purpose
that I understand very little of. Maybe 1,500 miles later I am
wiser, less frightened, and more home. But for now, I need to be
comfortable running simply with the questions in my heart.

JULY 14, 2016

I found the above in my digital diary just as I finished writing this book. It was the first entry I had ever tagged with #wayofgentlepower. At that point in my life, I didn't know I would write this book; my life revolved entirely around researching and speaking about sisu. I was still carrying a lot of pain from past wounds that prevented me from easing into life and understanding that suppleness is even stronger than sisu, and even more than nowadays, I was still learning to put presence over perfection.

In retrospect, that message was one of many that helped me learn a softer approach to strength—one that deemphasized force and encouraged curiosity. Even with a worthy goal in mind—like transforming leadership or making the world a better place—it's important to let go of specific goals and timelines. Just as we can't open a flower or make birds sing on command, gentle power can't be forced. Gentle power is never forced.

Whether I ran, walked, or sat in silence, I had to first learn to love the questions, the uncertainty, and the incompleteness of everything in my life. That's still how I find my tender fulfillment—in the path itself. The answers eventually lose their urgency and most of their importance. To me, it comes down to learning to slow down and letting go of grasping so much. To feel the gravel of the proverbial path under my bare feet—the the present moment as it is—is an end itself. It's these incremental shifts that at first seem like nothing, but which over time, amount to an entirely new reality.

The world as we know it is straining under the current transformations in different arenas of human life—political, social, medical, environmental, technological, and so on. Within this, we're confronted with urgency, but also an incredible opportunity to explore the boundaries of our known reality. Be it in athletics, activism, parenthood, or inner awareness, the ways in which we continue to engage life with truth and goodness are what promises such hope for our future.

Sisu is the hidden strength we find after we reach the edges of our assumed capacities. It is the next breath, step, and heartbeat, or the seemingly impossible action taken when the scale could easily tip either way. Neither sisu nor systems intelligence alone is enough to deliver us to the other side of our global challenges, but if we can combine these two and envelope them in gentle power, we can create a cycle of integrity-fueled fortitude to carry us forward.

Our human family consists of about eight billion leaders. Each of us plays a vital role in the collective transformation that the world is calling for. It all starts in our own heart, in our own gentle power. Look around—you're not alone. Look down—the earth holds you up. Look up—there's vastness and magic everywhere. Look within—you hold the keys.

Acknowledgments

To paraphrase Isaac Newton, whatever diamonds you find hidden in these pages are because I stand on the shoulders of giants. These (gentle) giants represent an entire cosmos of people and are, thus, far too many to name. They include people like John, a homeless man I met in a busy crossroad in New York City who taught me about gentle power through his infectious smile that reflected his trust in life. They also include spontaneous conversations with both locals and kung fu masters alike in China about the foundational nature of yin and yang; my parents in Finland; various mentors from academia, martial arts, and spirituality; and luminaries I've never met, like William James and Etty Hillesum, whose mentorship I would have cherished for their paramount understanding of inner fortitude. That said, I would like to acknowledge a number of real-life alchemists whose thoughts, support, or ways of being have been seminal to my journey of bringing this book to life.

Warm thank you to my majestic editor Robert Lee who simply *gets me*. To the Sounds True family: Diana Ventimiglia, Sahar Al-Nima, Mitchell Clute, Lauren Szmyd, and Tami Simon for creating the most welcoming home for *Gentle Power* that I could have imagined. To the design team for the sublime cover (inspired by the Japanese kintsugi) that makes my heart quiver every time I look at it. To my sharp Finnish literary agent Elina Ahlbäck and her team for their enthusiasm, as well as to Rhea Lyons for invaluable help with the book proposal.

A loving thank you to my mentor and supervisor extraordinaire Esa Saarinen and Pipsa the Queen for their love and ongoing guidance. To Lauri Järvilehto, Frank Martela, Angela Duckworth, Marty Seligman, James Pawelski, Emma Seppälä, and Scott Barry Kaufman whose presence, encouragement, and good favor ushered me onward in the early stages of the research and continue to do so. To Aaron Jarden, Sherri

Fisher, Lisa Samson, Leona Brandwene, Kathryn H. Britton, Carin Rockind, and Robert Easton for their support and acts of kindness along the same journey.

Thank you to my mother Elisa and father Pertti, Hannele Katajamäki, and Eija Lahti for their lifelong benevolent witnessing and enduring love for me. To magical Ukko and Inkeri Kärkkäinen, Maria Jain, Johanna Matikka, Ritva Enäkoski, Saad Alayyoubi, Mariela Kleiner, Rossella Munafo, Georgia Shreve, Janur Yasa, Anna Emilia Pajari, Paula Mäkelä, Solveig Hägnas, Peter Kenttä, and Lauri Pietinalho for the example, companionship, and elevating role they have played in my humble pilgrimage into gentle power.

To Asta Raami, Anika Lichthenberg, Annastiina Hintsa, Pamela Prather, Leo Pakkhoo, Douglas Robin, Adrian Blackwood, Susan Blackwood, Kaisa Kärkkäinen, Ulrika Björkstam and Ida Tiilikainen for the wealth of inspiration and abundance of stirring conversations in the past. To Louis Alloro, Helen Tsim, Hunter Reynolds, Kevin Adler, Jean-François Ruiz, and Nelli Såger, as well as Stephane Leblanc and Hallie Gardner posthumously for their friendship and inspiration that has proved invaluable in guiding me to ask better questions and find more answers.

To Kentaro Toyama, Jane Dutton, Dean Karnazes, Norma Bastidas, Cindy Mason, Raimo Hämäläinen, Rick Smith, Ilmari Määttänen, Pentti Henttonen, Julius Väliaho, Paula Reed, Päivi Rissanen, Nico Rose, Travis Millman, Robert Nadeau Shihan, Richard Moon Sensei, RJ Singh, Lôc Le Van, Tim Lomas, and Todd Kashdan for their wisdom and work that inspired me greatly while doing research for the book.

To the most magical Mina and James Holder, Nicola Woodward and Percy McDonald, Colart, Sonja and Indigo Miles, Janelle Fletcher, Amy Willoughby, Victoria Jack, Mandy Reeve, Jup Brown, Lyn and Ronnie Brown, Belinda Jane, Liane Fujita-Ahmed, Rameez Ahmed, James Marriott, Jiří Janik, AJ Williams, Amritaa Ess, Chase Fleming, Petra Nylund, Ben Berkowitz, and Max Berkowitz for seeing me through the initiation of New Zealand with your love in action.

To every sisuesque person over the years who's shared their stories on sisu and gentle power; to my beautiful sisters and brothers who endured the unthinkable in its many forms but who are holding onto light—becoming lighthouses themselves, and to everyone out there who resonates with the *way of gentle power.*

When we join our hands and hearts, we can build an unshakeable foundation for the beautiful world that we know is possible—during our generation if we make it our priority. The journey continues!

Further Reading

The author was greatly inspired by the following books:

Marcus Aurelius Antoninus: *The Meditations of the Emperor Marcus Aurelius Antoninus*

Jason Digges: *Conflict = Energy: The Transformative Practice of Authentic Relating*

Adam Grant: *Give and Take: Why Helping Others Drives Our Success*

Raimo P. Hämäläinen and Esa Saarinen (eds.): *Systems Intelligence in Leadership and Everyday Life*

David Hawkins: *Power vs. Force: The Hidden Determinants of Human Behavior*

William James: *The Energies of Men*

Todd B. Kashdan: *The Art of Insubordination: How to Dissent and Defy Effectively*

Scott Barry Kaufman: *Transcend: The New Science of Self-Actualization*

Diane Poole Heller: *The Power of Attachment: How to Create Deep and Lasting Intimate Relationships*

Emma Seppälä: *The Happiness Track: How to Apply the Science of Happiness to Accelerate Your Success*

Richard Strozzi-Heckler: *The Art of Somatic Coaching: Embodying Skillful Action, Wisdom, and Compassion*

Lao Tzu: *Tao Te Ching*

Notes

Epigraph

1. Peter A. Levine, *Waking the Tiger: Healing Trauma* (Berkeley, CA: North Atlantic Books, 1997).

Preface: An Invitation to Gentle Power

1. Martin Luther King, Jr., *Where Do We Go from Here: Chaos or Community?* (Boston, MA: Beacon Press, 1967).

Introduction

1. Hudson Strode, "Sisu: A Word That Explains Finland," *New York Times*, January 14, 1940, nytimes.com/1940/01/14/archives/sisu-a-word-that-explains-finland.html.

2. Oskari Tokoi, *Sisu: Even Through a Stone Wall* (New York: Robert Speller and Sons, 1957).

3. Damon Beres, "Most Honest Cities: The Reader's Digest 'Lost Wallet' Test," *Reader's Digest* (blog), August 26, 2018, rd.com/list/most-honest-cities-lost-wallet-test/.

Chapter 1: You Are the Leader Now

1. David Hawkins, *Power vs. Force: The Hidden Determinants of Human Behavior* (London, UK: Hay House, 2014).

2. Timothy D. Wilson, *Strangers to Ourselves: Discovering the Adaptive Unconscious* (Cambridge, MA: The Belknap Press of Harvard University Press, 2004).

3. Y. N. Harari, "In the Battle Against Coronavirus, Humanity Lacks Leadership," *Time*, March 15, 2020, time.com/5803225/yuval-noah-harari-coronavirus-humanity-leadership/.

4. Jason Digges, *Conflict = Energy: The Transformative Practice of Authentic Relating* (n.p.: ART International, 2020).

Chapter 2: Getting Over the Power Paralysis

1. Bertrand Russell, *Power: A New Social Analysis* (New York: Norton, 1938).

2. Abraham H. Maslow, *Personality and Growth: A Humanistic Psychologist in the Classroom* (Anna Maria, FL: Maurice Bassett, 2019).

3. Maslow, *Personality and Growth*, 334.

4. Maslow, *Personality and Growth*, 335.

5. Eric Liu, "Why Ordinary People Need to Understand Power," September 3, 2013, produced for TED.com, video, 17:06, ted.com/talks/eric_liu_why_ordinary_people_need_to_understand_power?language=en.

6. Rye Barcott, *It Happened on the Way to War: A Marine's Path to Peace* (New York: Bloomsbury, 2011).

7. N. E. Dunbar and J. K. Burgoon, "Perceptions of Power and Interactional Dominance in Interpersonal Relationships," *Journal of Social and Personal Relationships* 22 (2005): 207–233.

8. A. K. Farrell, J. A. Simpson, and A. J. Rothman, "The Relationship Power Inventory: Development and Validation," *Personal Relationships* 22 (2015): 387–413, semanticscholar.org/paper/The-relationship-power-inventory%3A-Development-and-Farrell-Simpson/a154e1dbe4ead673164d14f0b2a864e2132c0467.

9. J. R. P. French Jr. and B. H. Raven, "The Bases of Social Power," in *Studies in Social Power*, ed. D. Cartwright (Ann Arbor, MI: University of Michigan Press, 1959), 150–167.

10. Dacher Keltner, *The Power Paradox: How We Gain and Lose Influence* (New York: Penguin Books, 2016).

11. William James, "The Energies of Men," *Science* 25, no. 635 (1907): 321–332.

12. American Psychological Association, "Stress Effects on the Body," American Psychological Association (blog), November 1, 2018, apa.org/topics/stress/body.

13. I. Milosevic, S. Maric, and D. Loncar, "Defeating the Toxic Boss: The Nature of Toxic Leadership and the Role of Followers," *Journal of Leadership & Organizational Studies* 27, no. 2 (2019): 117–137, doi.org/10.1177/1548051819833374.

14. Jean Lipman-Blumen, *Toxic Leadership: A Conceptual Framework* (Claremont, CA: Claremont Graduate University, 2005).

15. John Paul Steele, "Antecedents and Consequences of Toxic Leadership in the U. S. Army: A Two Year Review and Recommended Solutions," *Center for Army Leadership* (June 2011): 1–37.

16. Milosevic, Maric, and Loncar, "Defeating the Toxic Boss."

17. Keltner, *The Power Paradox*, 2–3.

Chapter 3: Finding the Path

1. William Shakespeare, *As You Like It* (New York: Penguin Books, 2000).

2. Martin E. P. Seligman, *Authentic Happiness: Using the New Positive Psychology to Realize Your Potential for Lasting Fulfillment* (New York: Atria Books, 2002).

3. A. L. Duckworth, T. A. Steen, and M. E. P. Seligman, "Positive Psychology in Clinical Practice," *Annual Reviews of Clinical Psychology* 1 (2005): 629–651, doi.org/10.1146/annurev.clinpsy.1.102803 .144154; Martin E. P. Seligman and Mihalyi Csikszentmihalyi, "Positive Psychology: An Introduction," *American Psychologist* 55, no. 1 (2000): 5–1, doi.org/10.1037/0003-066X.55.1.5.

4. Duckworth, Steen, and Seligman, "Positive Psychology in Clinical Practice."

Chapter 4: The Paradox of Gentleness

1. This quote is widely attributed in various sources, mostly to Saint Francis de Sales and Ralph W. Stockman.

2. Melissa Nightingale, "Finnish Woman Emilia Lahti to Run 50 Ultramarathons in 50 Days in New Zealand," *New Zealand Herald*, January 11, 2018, nzherald.co.nz/nz/finnish-woman -emilia-lahti-to-run-50-ultramarathons-in-50-days-in-new-zealand /5DYJXB6DNVY4WIW6STNKSVIBDI.

3. André Comte-Sponville, *A Small Treatise on the Great Virtues: The Uses of Philosophy in Everyday Life* (New York: Henry Holt and Company, 2002), 186, 190.

4. Comte-Sponville, *A Small Treatise on the Great Virtues*, 186.

5. Brené Brown, *Dare to Lead: Brave Work. Tough Conversation. Whole Hearts.* (New York: Random House, 2018), 40.

6. Aristotle, *Aristotle in 23 Volumes*, vol. 19, trans. H. Rackham. (Cambridge, MA: Harvard University Press, 1934). Location of citation used: Nic. Eth, 1126a:6, data.perseus.org/citations /urn:cts:greekLit:tlg0086.tlg010.perseus-eng1:1126a.

7. Comte-Sponville, *A Small Treatise on the Great Virtues*, 186, 190.

8. Marcus Aurelius Antoninus, *Meditations of the Emperor Marcus Aurelius*, trans. Arthur Spenser Loat Farquharson (London, UK: Oxford University Press, 1944), book XI.

9. Anne Dufourmantelle, *The Power of Gentleness: Meditations on the Risk of Living* (New York: Fordham University Press, 2018).

10. Rainer Maria Rilke, *Letters to a Young Poet*, trans. M. D. Herter Norton (New York: W. W. Norton and Co., 2004).

11. Hazelden Betty Ford Foundation, "ABA, Hazelden Betty Ford Foundation Release First National Study on Attorney Substance Use,"

press release, February 3, 2016, hazeldenbettyford.org /about-us/news-media/press-release/2016-aba-hazelden-release -first-study-attorney-substance-use.

12. Amy Edmondson, *The Fearless Organization: Creating Psychological Safety in the Workplace for Learning, Innovation, and Growth* (Hoboken, NJ: Wiley & Sons, 2018).

13. Edmondson, *The Fearless Organization*, 107.

14. J. M. Lilius, et al., "Understanding Compassion Capability," *Human Relations* 64, no. 7 (2011): 873–899, doi.org/10.1177 /0018726710396250.

15. Personal email exchange with Jane Dutton on October 14, 2021.

Chapter 5: The Science of the Good Heart

1. Emma Seppälä and Kim Cameron, "The Best Leaders Have a Contagious Positive Energy," Harvard Business Review, April 18, 2022, hbr.org/2022/04/the-best-leaders-have-a-contagious-positive-energy.

2. Daniel Goleman, "How Empathy Adds to a Leader's Power," Korn Ferry (blog), kornferry.com/insights/this-week-in-leadership/how -empathy-adds-to-a-leaders-power.

3. Joan Marques, "Understanding the Strength of Gentleness: Soft-Skilled Leadership on the Rise," *Journal of Business Ethics* 116, no. 1 (2013): 163–171, doi.org/10.1007/S10551-012-1471-7.

4. Lao Tzu, *Tao Te Ching*, trans. James Legge, Sacred Books of the East, vol 39, 1891. sacred-texts.com/tao/taote.htm.

5. Andrea Appleton, "Cultivating Creativity," *Think* (Spring/Summer 2014), case.edu/think/spring2014/cultivating-creativity.html# .YfYuFPVBy3I.

6. J. E. Dutton, J. Lilius, and J. Kanov, "The Transformative Potential of Compassion at Work," in *Handbook of Transformative Cooperation: New Designs and Dynamics*, eds. S. Piderit, R. Fry, and D. Cooperrider (Stanford, CA: Stanford University Press, 2007), 107–126; Clifton B. Parker, "Compassion Is a Wise and Effective

Managerial Strategy, Stanford Expert Says," Stanford News
Service, May 21, 2015, news.stanford.edu/pr/2015/pr-compassion
-workplace-seppala-052115.html.

7. Charles Duhigg, "What Google Learned from Its Quest to Build
the Perfect Team," *New York Times Magazine*, February 25, 2016,
nytimes.com/2016/02/28/magazine/what-google-learned-from-its
-quest-to-build-the-perfect-team.html?smid=pl-share.

8. Edmondson, *The Fearless Organization*.

9. Amy C. Edmondson and Z. Lei, "Psychological Safety: The History,
Renaissance, and Future of an Interpersonal Construct," *Annual
Review of Organizational Psychology and Organizational Behavior* 1
(2014): 23–43, doi.org/10.1146/annurev-orgpsych-031413-091305.

10. Amy C. Edmondson, "The Local and Variegated Nature of Learning
in Organizations," *Organization Science* 13, no. 2 (2002): 128–146.

11. Gareth Cook, "Why We Are Wired to Connect," *Scientific American*,
October 22, 2013, scientificamerican.com/article/why-we-are
-wired-to-connect/.

12. G. Šimić, et al., "Understanding Emotions: Origins and Roles of the
Amygdala," *Biomolecules* 11, no. 6 (2021): 823, doi.org/10.3390
/biom11060823.

13. Sage Media, "The ROI of Psychological Safety - Sage Advice:
Episode 50," video, August 13, 2019, youtube.com/watch?v=
a6pbDLHtNFM.

14. Brian Clark Howard, "Could Malcolm Gladwell's Theory of Cockpit
Culture Apply to Asiana Crash?" *National Geographic*, July 11,
2013, nationalgeographic.com/adventure/article/130709-asiana
-flight-214-crash-korean-airlines-culture-outliers.

15. Howard, "Could Malcolm Gladwell's Theory of Cockpit Culture
Apply to Asiana Crash?"

16. Karen Kangas Dwyer and Marlina M. Davidson, "Is Public Speaking
Really More Feared Than Death?" *Communication Research Reports*

29, no. 2 (2012): 99–107, tandfonline.com/doi/abs/10.1080 /08824096.2012.667772.

17. Jean Decety Martineau and Eric Racine, "Social Neuroscience of Empathy and Its Implication for Business Ethics," in *Organizational Neuroethics: Reflections on the Contributions of Neuroscience to Management Theories and Business Practices*, eds. Jean Decety Martineau and Eric Racine (Cham, Switzerland: Springer, 2020), researchgate.net/publication/337605830_The_Social_Neuroscience _of_Empathy_and_Its_Implication_for_Business_Ethics.

18. Matt Trainer, "Strong Leadership Is Gentle," Medium (blog), medium .com/the-mission/strong-leadership-is-gentle-4c1e9f69df65.

19. Anne Dufourmantelle, *The Power of Gentleness: Meditations on the Risk of Living* (New York: Fordham University Press, 2018), 22.

20. Barbara L. Fredrickson, "What Good Are Positive Emotions?" *Review of General Psychology* 2, no. 3 (September 1, 1998): 300–319, doi.org/10.1037/1089-2680.2.3.300.

21. Julie Ray, "Americans' Stress, Worry, and Anger Intensified in 2018," Gallup, April 25, 2019, news.gallup.com/poll/249098/americans -stress-worry-anger-intensified-2018.aspx.

22. The American Institute of Stress, "Workplace Stress,"stress.org /workplace-stress; Korn Ferry, "Worried Workers: Korn Ferry Survey Finds Professionals Are More Stressed Out at Work Today Than 5 Years Ago," November 8, 2018, kornferry.com/about-us /press/worried-workers-korn-ferry-survey-finds-professionals-are -more-stressed-out-at-work-today-than-5-years-ago.

23. American Psychological Association, "Stress in the Workplace Survey Summary," PowerPoint presentation, March 2011, apa.org/news /press/releases/phwa-survey-summary.pdf.

24. Jane E. Dutton, "Fostering High Quality Connections Through Respectful Engagement," *Stanford Social Innovation Review* (Winter 2003): 54–57, researchgate.net/publication/262725459_The _Power_of_High_Quality_Connections.

25. Dutton, "Fostering High Quality Connections Through Respectful Engagement."

26. Jane. E. Dutton and Emily D. Heaphy, "The Power of High-Quality Connections," in *Positive Organizational Scholarship*, eds. K. S. Cameron, J. E. Dutton, and R. E. Quinn (San Francisco, CA: Berrett-Koehler Publishers, 2003), 263–278, researchgate.net/publication /262725459_The_Power_of_High_Quality_Connections.

27. Michael Prinzing, et al., "Staying 'in Sync' with Others During COVID-19: Perceived Positivity Resonance Mediates Cross-Sectional and Longitudinal Links Between Trait Resilience and Mental Health," *The Journal of Positive Psychology* (2020), doi.org /10.1080/17439760.2020.1858336.

28. Diane Poole Heller, *The Power of Attachment: How to Create Deep and Lasting Intimate Relationships* (Boulder, CO: Sounds True, 2019).

29. John Bowlby, *Attachment and Loss: Attachment*, vol. 1 (New York: Basic Books, 1969).

30. Cindy Hazan and Philip R. Shaver, "Love and Work: An Attachment-Theoretical Perspective," *Journal of Personality and Social Psychology* 59, no. 2 (1990): 270–280, doi.org/10.1037/0022 -3514.59.2.270.

31. Cindy Hazan and Philip R. Shaver, "Romantic Love Conceptualized as an Attachment Process," *Journal of Personality and Social Psychology* 52, no. 3 (1987): 511–524, doi.org/10.1037/0022-3514.52.3.511.

Chapter 6: The Serendipitous Road to Sisu

1. Ralph Waldo Emerson, *Journals of Ralph Waldo Emerson, with Annotations - 1841–1844* (Pittsburgh, PA: Mellon Press, 2007).

2. William James, "The Energies of Men," Science 25, no. 635 (1907).

3. André Comte-Sponville, *A Small Treatise on the Great Virtues: The Uses of Philosophy in Everyday Life* (New York: Henry Holt and Company, 2002), 45.

4. René Descartes, *The Passions of the Soul and Other Late Philosophical Writings*, ed. M. Moriarty (Oxford, UK: Oxford University Press, 2015).

5. Marcus Aurelius, *The Meditations of the Emperor Marcus Aurelius Antoninus*, trans. George Long (New York: The Chesterfield Society, 1862).

6. Richard G. Tedeschi, et al., *Posttraumatic Growth: Theory, Research, and Applications* (New York: Routledge, 2018).

Chapter 7: The Three Essences of Sisu

1. Emily Dickinson, "A Death Blow Is a Life Blow to Some," 1866, en.wikisource.org/wiki/A_Death_blow_is_a_Life_blow_to_Some.

2. Emilia Elisabet Lahti, "Embodied Fortitude: An Introduction to the Finnish Construct of Sisu," *International Journal of Wellbeing* 9, no. 1 (2019): 61–82, doi.org/10.5502/ijw.v9i1.672.

3. A. Pollo, E. Carlino, and F. Benedetti, "The Top-Down Influence of Ergogenic Placebos on Muscle Work and Fatigue," *The European Journal of Neuroscience* 28, no. 2 (2008): 379–388, doi.org/10.1111/j.1460-9568.2008.06344.x.

4. V. R. Clark, et al., "Placebo Effect of Carbohydrate Feedings During a 40-km Cycling Time Trial," *Medicine and Science in Sports and Exercise* 32, no. 9 (2000): 1642–1647, doi.org/10.1097/00005768-200009000-00019.

5. Antonella Pollo, et al., "Placebo Mechanisms Across Different Conditions: From the Clinical Setting to Physical Performance," *Philosophical Transactions of the Royal Society of London. Series B* 366 (2011): 1790–1798, doi.org/10.1098/rstb.2010.0381.

6. Angela Duckworth and James J. Gross, 2014. "Self-Control and Grit: Related but Separable Determinants of Success," *Current Directions in Psychological Science* 23, no. 5 (2014): 319–325, doi.org/10.1177/0963721414541462.

7. P. Carroll and J. A. Shepperd, "Preparedness, Mental Simulations, and Future Outlooks," in *Handbook of Imagination and Mental Simulation*, eds. K. D. Markman, W. M. P. Klein, and J. A. Suhr (New York: Psychology Press, 2009), 425–440.

8. V. Job, et al., "Implicit Theories About Willpower Predict Self-Regulation and Grades in Everyday Life," *Journal of Personality and Social Psychology* 108, no. 4 (2015): 637–647, doi.org/10.1037/pspp0000014.

9. R. Rosenthal and L. Jacobsen, *Pygmalion in the Classroom: Teacher Expectation and Pupils' Intellectual Development* (New York: Holt, Rinehart, and Winston, 1968).

10. R. Rosenthal and E. Y. Babad, "Pygmalion in the Gymnasium," *Educational Leadership* 43, no. 1 (1985): 36–39.

11. V. Job, C. S. Dweck, and G. M. Walton, "Ego Depletion—Is It All in Your Head? Implicit Theories About Willpower Affect Self-Regulation," *Psychological Science* 21, no. 11 (2010): 1686–1693, doi.org/10.1177/0956797610384745.

12. Albert Camus, "A Return to Tipasa," in *Lyrical and Critical Essays*, ed. Philip Thody and trans. Ellen Conroy Kennedy (New York: Vintage Books, 1970).

13. Peter A. Levine, *Waking the Tiger: Healing Trauma* (Berkeley, CA: North Atlantic Books, 1997).

14. Thomas Hanna, "What Is Somatics?," Clincial Somatics, somatics.org/library/htl-wis1.

15. Marcus Aurelius, *The Meditations of the Emperor Marcus Aurelius Antoninus*, trans. George Long (New York: The Chesterfield Society, 1862).

16. Maija Länsimäki, "Suomalaista Sisua [Finnish Sisu]," March 11, 2003, *Helsingin Sanomat*.

17. George Gilbert Ramsay, *Juvenial and Persius* (New York: G. P. Putnam's Sons, 1920).

18. A. A. Kousoulis, et al., "From the 'Hungry Acid' to Pepsinogen: A Journey Through Time in Quest for the Stomach's Secretion," *Annals of Gastroenterology* 25, no. 2 (2012), 119–122.

19. T. G. Dinan, et al., "Collective Unconscious: How Gut Microbes Shape Human Behavior," *Journal of Psychiatric Research 63* (2015): 1–9; J. A. Foster, L. Rinaman, and J. F. Cryan, "Stress and the Gut-Brain Axis: Regulation by the Microbiome," *Neurobiology of Stress 7* (2017): 124–136, doi.org/10.1016/j.ynstr.2017.03.001.

20. P. Bercik, et al., "The Intestinal Microbiota Affect Central Levels of Brain-Derived Neurotropic Factor and Behavior in Mice," *Gastroenterology* 141, no. 2 (2011): 599–609.e1-3; J. A. Bravo, et al., "Ingestion of Lactobacillus Strain Regulates Emotional Behavior and Central GABA Receptor Expression in a Mouse via the Vagus Nerve," *Proceedings of the National Academy of Sciences* 108, no. 38 (2011): 16050–16055.

21. Bercik, et al., "The Intestinal Microbiota Affect Central Levels of Brain-Derived Neurotropic Factor and Behavior in Mice."

22. D.-W. Kang, et al., "Microbiota Transfer Therapy Alters Gut Ecosystem and Improves Gastrointestinal and Autism Symptoms: An Open-Label Study," *Microbiome 5*, no. 1 (2017): 10.

23. Lorena Lobo, et al., "The History and Philosophy of Ecological Psychology," *Frontiers in Psychology* 9 (November 27, 2018), doi.org /10.3389/fpsyg.2018.02228.

24. A. D. Wilson and S. Golonka, "Embodied Cognition Is Not What You Think It Is," *Frontiers in Psychology* 4, no. 58 (2013): 1–13, doi.org/10.3389/fpsyg.2013.00058.

25. Jackie D. Wood, "Enteric Nervous System: Brain-in-the-Gut," in *Physiology of the Gastrointestinal Tract*, 6th ed., ed. H. M. Said (Cambridge, MA: Academic Press, 2018), 361–372, doi.org/10 .1016/B978-0-12-809954-4.00015-3.

Chapter 8: The Shadow of Sisu

1. Jalal al-Din Rumi, *The Essential Rumi*, trans. Coleman Barks (San Francisco, CA: Harper), 174.

2. Scott Barry Kaufman, *Transcend: The New Science of Self-Actualization* (New York: TarcherPerigee, 2020), xxv.

3. P. Henttonen, et al., "A Measure for Assessment of Beneficial and Harmful Fortitude: Development and Initial Validation of the Sisu Scale," *PsyArXiv*, January 25, 2022, doi.org/10.31234/osf.io/7nptw.

Chapter 9: Know the Tough, Live from the Soft

1. Bruce R. Linnell, trans., *Dao De Jing: A Minimalist Translation* (Project Gutenberg eBook, 2015), gutenberg.org/files/49965/49965-h/49965-h.htm.

2. Esther Hillesum, *The Letters and Diaries of Etty Hillesum, 1941–1943*, trans. Arnold J. Pomerans and ed. Klaas A. D. Smelik (Grand Rapids, MI: William B. Eerdmans Publishing Company, 1986).

3. Anna Aluffi Pentinini, "A Woman's All-Embracing Search of 'the Other': Etty Hillesum as the Basis of a 'Pedagogy of Care and Attention,'" in *Reading Etty Hillesum in Context: Writings, Life, and Influences of a Visionary Author*, eds. Klaas Smelik, Gerrit Van Oord, and Jurjen Wiersma (Amsterdam, Netherlands: Amsterdam University Press, 2018).

4. David R. Hawkins, *Power vs. Force: The Hidden Determinants of Human Behavior* (London, UK: Hay House, 2014), 133.

5. Susan Perry, *Remembering O-Sensei: Living and Training with Morihei Ueshiba, Founder of Aikido* (Boston, MA: Shambhala Publications, 2002).

6. Lao Tzu, *Tao Te Ching*, trans. James Legge, Sacred Books of the East, vol 39, 1891. sacred-texts.com/ta/taote.htm.

7. Martin Luther King, Jr., *Where Do We Go from Here: Chaos or Community?* (Boston, MA: Beacon Press, 1967), 38.

8. Barbara L. Fredrickson, "Love: Positivity Resonance as a Fresh, Evidence-Based Perspective on an Age-Old Topic," in *Handbook of Emotions*, 4th ed., eds. L. F. Barrett, M. Lewis, and J. M. Haviland (New York: Guilford Press, 2016), 847–858.

9. M. Ueshiba, *The Art of Peace*, trans. John Stevens. (Boston, MA: Shambhala Publications, 1992), 45.

10. Daniele Bolelli, *On the Warrior's Path: Philosophy, Fighting, and Martial Arts Mythology*, 2nd ed. (Berkeley, CA: Blue Snake Books, 2008).

11. Hillesum, *The Letters and Diaries of Etty Hillesum, 1941–1943*, 535.

Chapter 10: Self-Worth

1. Carl Jung, *C. G. Jung Letters, Volume I, 1906–1950*, eds. Gerhard Adler and Aniela Jaffé (New York: Routledge, 1973), 33.

2. Oriah Mountaindreamer, *The Invitation* (San Francisco, CA: HarperOne, 1999).

Chapter 11: Gentle Power and Society

1. Charlie Chaplin, *The Great Dictator* (Charles Chaplin Film Corporation, 1940).

2. J. H. Fowler and Nicholas. A. Christakis, "Dynamic Spread of Happiness in a Large Social Network: Longitudinal Analysis Over 20 Years in the Framingham Heart Study," *BMJ* 337 (December 3, 2008): a2338, doi.org/10.1136/bmj.a2338.

3. Phone interview with Kentaro Toyama on September 21, 2021.

4. Email communication with Cindy Mason on October 15, 2021.

5. Jeremy Heimans and Henry Timms, *New Power: How Anyone Can Persuade, Mobilize, and Succeed in Our Chaotic, Connected Age* (New York: Doubleday, 2018).

6. I. Grossmann, B. K. Sahdra, and J. Ciarrochi, "A Heart and a Mind: Self-Distancing Facilitates the Association Between Heart

Rate Variability, and Wise Reasoning," *Frontiers in Behavioral Neuroscience* 10 (2016), doi.org/10.3389/fnbeh.2016.00068.

7. Thea von Harbou, *Metropolis,* directed by Fritz Lang (Germany: UFA, 1927), imdb.com/title/tt0017136/.

Chapter 12: Sadhana (What Every Leader Needs)

1. Esther Hillesum, *The Letters and Diaries of Etty Hillesum,* 1941–1943, trans. Arnold J. Pomerans and ed. Klaas A. D. Smelik (Grand Rapids, MI: William B. Eerdmans Publishing Company, 1986).

2. William James, "The Energies of Men," Science 25, no. 635 (1907).

3. Philippa Lally, et al., "How Are Habits Formed: Modelling Habit Formation in the Real World," *European Journal of Social Psychology* 40 (2010): 998–1009.

4. John R. Hayes, "Cognitive Processes in Creativity, Occasional Paper No. 18," in *Handbook of Creativity, Assessment, Research, and Theory,* eds. John A. Glover, Royce R. Ronning, and Cecil R. Reynolds (New York: Plenum Publishing Corporation, 1989).

5. K. A. Ericsson, R. T. Krampe, and C. Tesch-Tomer, "The Role of Deliberate Practice in the Acquisition of Expert Performance," *Psychological Review* 100, no. 3 (1993): 363–406.

6. K. A. Ericsson and K. W. Harwell, "Deliberate Practice and Proposed Limits on the Effects of Practice on the Acquisition of Expert Performance: Why the Original Definition Matters and Recommendations for Future Research," *Frontiers in Psychology* 25 (October 2019), doi.org/10.3389/fpsyg.2019.02396.

7. K. A. Ericsson and R. Pool, *Peak: Secrets from the New Science of Expertise* (New York: Houghton Mifflin & Harcourt, 2016); Ericsson and Harwell, "Deliberate Practice and Proposed Limits on the Effects of Practice on the Acquisition of Expert Performance."

8. Juliette Tocino-Smith, "What Is Eustress? A Look at the Psychology and Benefits" *PositivePsychology.com* (blog), January 15, 2019, positivepsychology.com/what-is-eustress/.

9. Julie A. Markham and William T. Greenough, "Experience-Driven Brain Plasticity: Beyond the Synapse," *Neuron Glia Biology* 1, no. 4 (2004): 351–363, doi.org/10.1017/s1740925x05000219.

10. Rick Hanson, "How to Grow the Good in Your Brain," *Berkeley Greater Good Magazine* (blog), September 24, 2013, greatergood .berkeley.edu/article/item/how_to_grow_the_good_in_your_brain.

11. L. Petrosini, et al., "On Whether the Environmental Enrichment May Provide Cognitive and Brain Reserves," *Brain Research Reviews* 61, no. 2 (October 2009): 221–239, doi.org/10.1016/j.brainresrev .2009.07.002; Jeffrey M. Schwartz and Sharon Begley, *The Mind and the Brain: Neuroplasticity and the Power of Mental Force* (New York: Regan Books/Harper Collins Publishers, 2002).

12. Schwartz and Begley, *The Mind and the Brain.*

Chapter 13: Systems Intelligence Leadership

1. Anne Dufourmantelle, *The Power of Gentleness: Meditations on the Risk of Living.*

2. David Bohm and Mark Edwards, *Changing Consciousness: Exploring the Hidden Source of Social, Political, and Environmental Crises Facing Our World* (New York: Harper, 1991).

3. Edward O. Wilson, *The Social Conquest of Earth* (New York: Liveright, 2012).

4. Karen Golden-Biddle, "Create Micro-Moves for Organizational Change," in *How to Be a Positive Leader: Small Actions, Big Impact*, eds. J. E. Dutton and G. M. Spreitzer (San Francisco, CA: Berrett-Koehler, 2014).

5. Martha. S. Feldman and Anne Khademian, "Empowerment and Cascading Vitality," in *Positive Organizational Scholarship*, eds. K. S. Cameron, J. E. Dutton, and R.E. Quinn (San Francisco, CA: Berrett-Koehler, 2003): 343–358.

6. Raimo P. Hämäläinen and Esa Saarinen, "Systems Intelligent Leadership," in *Systems Intelligence in Leadership and Everyday Life*, eds. R. P. Hämäläinen and E. Saarinen (Espoo, Finland: Systems Analysis Laboratory, Helsinki University of Technology, 2007).

7. Raimo Hämäläinen, Rachel Jones, and Esa Saarinen, *Being Better Better: Living with Systems Intelligence* (Helsinki, Finland: CreateSpace Independent Publishing Platform, 2014).

8. Esa Saarinen and Raimo P. Hämäläinen, eds., *Systems Intelligence: Discovering a Hidden Competence in Human Action and Organizational Life*, Helsinki University of Technology, Systems Analysis Laboratory, Research Reports A88, October 2004.

9. John M. Gottman, et al., *Mathematics of Marriage: Dynamic Nonlinear Models* (Cambridge, MA: The MIT Press/A Bradford Book, 2002), 88.

10. Rick Hanson, "How to Grow the Good in Your Brain," *Berkeley Greater Good Magazine* (blog), September 24, 2013, greatergood .berkeley.edu/article/item/how_to_grow_the_good_in_your_brain.

11. Hämäläinen and Saarinen, "Systems Intelligent Leadership."

12. Peter Senge, "Systems Thinking for a Better World," Aalto Systems Forum, 2014, video, youtube.com/watch?v=0QtQqZ6Q5-o.

13. James E. M. Watson, et al., "Catastrophic Declines in Wilderness Areas Undermine Global Environment Targets," *Current Biology* 26, no. 21 (2016): 2929–2934, doi.org/10.1016/j.cub.2016.08.049.

14. Hämäläinen and Saarinen, "Systems Intelligent Leadership."

Chapter 14: The Alchemy of Gentle Power

1. Alice Calaprice, *The Ultimate Quotable Einstein* (Princeton, NJ: Princeton University Press, 2011).

2. Lao Tzu, *Tao Te Ching*, trans. James Legge, Sacred Books of the East, vol 39, 1891. sacred-texts.com/ta/taote.htm.

3. Email interview with Dean Karnazes on October 22, 2021.

4. Kate Carter, "Ultra-Distance Runner Damian Hall on Setting a New Record: 'I Recommend a Daily Sob,'" *The Guardian*, June 7, 2016, theguardian.com/lifeandstyle/the-running-blog/2016/jun/07/damian-hall-new-record-i-recommend-a-daily-sob-south-west-coast-path-swcp.

5. Phone interview with Päivi Rissanen on September 9, 2021; Päivi Rissanen, "A Hopeless Case? An Autoethnography of Getting Mentally Ill and Re-habilitation of It," 2015, unpublished doctoral dissertation, University of Helsinki, helda.helsinki.fi/handle/10138/157106?locale-attribute=en.

6. Adam Grant, "We Don't Have to Fight Loneliness Alone," WorkLife with Adam Grant (podcast), April 2020, ted.com/talks/worklife_with_adam_grant_we_don_t_have_to_fight_loneliness_alone.

7. The American Institute of Stress, "42 Worrying Workplace Stress Statistics," September 25, 2019, stress.org/42-worrying-workplace-stress-statistics.

8. Infographics, DomesticShelters.org, domesticshelters.org/resources/statistics#.V2cn0eYrK35.

9. Design Within Reach, "Alvar Aalto," dwr.com/designer-alvar-aalto?lang=en_US.

10. V. K. Chattu, et al., "The Global Problem of Insufficient Sleep and Its Serious Public Health Implications," *Healthcare* 7, no. 1 (2018): 1, doi.org/10.3390/healthcare7010001.

11. B. K. Hölzel, et al., "Mindfulness Practice Leads to Increases in Regional Brain Gray Matter Density," *Psychiatry Research* 191, no. 1 (2011): 36–43, doi.org/10.1016/j.pscychresns.2010.08.006.

About the Author

EMILIA ELISABET LAHTI (PhD), who goes by Elisabet, is an awarded educator, applied psychology researcher, and founder of Sisu Lab that helps create communities and work cultures based on everyday leadership as an expression of courage and compassion. Her passion lies in discovering paths to the artful union of science and spirituality for everyday use.

Elisabet holds a master's degree in social psychology from the University of Tampere in Finland and a master's in applied positive psychology from the University of Pennsylvania, where she studied under Professors Martin Seligman and Angela Duckworth. Since initiating the research on the Finnish construct of sisu in 2012, Elisabet's doctoral work has involved exploring the limits of her own sisu through ultra-endurance running and Eastern martial arts, as well as a series of personal transformations and spiritual quests.

Her work on sisu has been featured by *The New Yorker*, Business Insider, BBC, *Forbes*, and more. Born and raised in Finland, she has lived and taught internationally and given talks at Fortune 500 companies, TEDx, Stanford University, and UC Berkeley. Elisabet is the founding member of the Positive Psychology Association of Finland as well as the creator of the nonprofit Sisu Not Silence that aims to promote action and research around nonviolence and active compassion in all domains of life. In 2018, Elisabet completed a 50-day/1,500-mile run and bicycle journey across the length of New Zealand to celebrate the strength of overcomers of interpersonal violence and present a series of in-person events throughout the journey to support the creation of cultures with zero tolerance to abuse in any shape or form.

Her personal life mission involves being a catalyst for connection and compassion, while acknowledging that doing so, ultimately, is but an intimate and honest dialogue with one's own heart. For more, visit sisulab.com.

About Sounds True

SOUNDS TRUE is a multimedia publisher whose mission is to inspire and support personal transformation and spiritual awakening. Founded in 1985 and located in Boulder, Colorado, we work with many of the leading spiritual teachers, thinkers, healers, and visionary artists of our time. We strive with every title to preserve the essential "living wisdom" of the author or artist. It is our goal to create products that not only provide information to a reader or listener but also embody the quality of a wisdom transmission.

For those seeking genuine transformation, Sounds True is your trusted partner. At SoundsTrue.com you will find a wealth of free resources to support your journey, including exclusive weekly audio interviews, free downloads, interactive learning tools, and other special savings on all our titles.

To learn more, please visit SoundsTrue.com/freegifts or call us toll-free at 800.333.9185.

sounds true
WAKING UP THE WORLD